The Book of Proverbs

Wisdom for Life

Maureen Schaffer

ໜ Foreword ໕

The Book of Proverbs contains wisdom for our lives. It is written in various literary ways. There are contrasts, comparisons, warnings, and explanations of results and consequences.

God created us to enjoy this life and it is by His wisdom we can avoid unnecessary troubles and have a much smoother experience. Decisions and priorities define our lives. The Book of Proverbs is designed to instruct and direct us in the practical areas of life.

Our Heavenly Father knows the wisest way to live and has given us instructions so our lives are built in a way that can function at their best as much as depends on us.

Wisdom guards us from unnecessary destruction and pain. The Book of Proverbs gives us advice that is able to be implemented with sweet results.

I pray as you peruse through Proverbs you will enjoy learning from your heavenly Father and choose the way of wisdom. This will bring Him glory and bring you great satisfaction.

ໜ Maureen

ೞ Why ೞ

The proverbs of Solomon the son of David, king of Israel; To know wisdom and instruction; to perceive the words of understanding; To receive the instruction of wisdom, justice, and judgment, and equity; To give life-wisdom to those who have yet to experience certain things, to the young man knowledge and discretion.

A wise man will hear, and will increase learning; and a man of understanding shall attain to wise counsels: To understand a proverb, and the interpretation; the words of the wise, and their dark sayings.

Proverbs 1:1-6

These proverbs are given to us that we might know wisdom. This would lead us to conclude we don't have wisdom or instruction of our own. They are also given that we might perceive the words of understanding. Words of understanding may have been given to us, yet we might not have perceived them as wise or valuable. Proverbs are also written to give us knowledge and discretion.

Proverbs were written to give us knowledge about money, relationships, work, child-rearing, sleep, our words, and a myriad of other subjects.

Solomon lets us know wisdom is important for any leadership role. Listening and taking heed to the wisdom of God will help us withstand the guaranteed onslaught of winds, rain, and floods of pressures and challenges that threaten quality of life. God knows wisdom builds lives that can be observed as sure, consistent, and built up to code — *His* code.

ࢾ Hear ࡸ

The fear of the LORD is the beginning of knowledge: but fools despise wisdom and instruction. My son, hear the instruction of your father, and do not forsake the law of your mother: For they shall be an ornament of grace to your head, and chains about your neck.

Proverbs 1:7-9

To even begin to know *anything* about ourselves, others, or life in general, we must have the fear of the Lord. We must be more concerned about His approval than any others' and His conclusions more than our own understanding or this world's conclusions.

When we are under our parents' care, we are to obey, knowing parental authority is given by God. Even as adults, parental instructions are to be esteemed as valuable advice.

Long after we grow up, our parents' instruction lingers in our character. When we hear the voice of our parents within us reminding us to get to bed, put on a jacket, or get those dishes done, we can enjoy the parental influence the Lord is still using to be an ornament upon our lives.

Listening to those above us in rank will *accessorize* our character just as the right jewelry ties an outfit together.

ఴ Refrain ಞ

*My son, if sinners entice you, do not consent. If they
say, Come with us, let us lay wait for blood, let us lurk
secretly for the innocent without cause: Let us swallow
them up alive as the grave; and whole, as those that go
down into the pit: We shall find all precious substance,
we shall fill our houses with spoil: Cast in your lot
among us; let us all have one purse: My son, do not
walk in the way with them; refrain your foot from their
path: For their feet run to evil, and make haste to shed
blood. Surely the net is spread for nothing in the sight
of any bird. And they lay wait for their own blood; they
lurk secretly for their own lives. So are the ways of
every one that is greedy of gain; which takes away the
life of the owners thereof.*

Proverbs 1:10-19

Money-making schemes are a dime a dozen. Many
times people will call us on the phone, appear on an
infomercial, or send an internet invitation to recruit
us to "get rich quick'. Believer, be careful! The Lord
warns us in 1 Timothy 6:10, *"For the love of money is
the root of all evil: which while some coveted after, they
have erred from the faith, and pierced themselves
through with many sorrows."* In Proverbs 15:27a it says,
"He that is greedy of gain troubles his own house..." We
must be content and seek first His kingdom and true
spiritual riches. This will help us avoid traps that rob
our lives of the peace God wants us to have. We will
end up with lives that are troubled, discontent, and
entangled in greed. This can rob us of the very lives
the Lord wants us to experience.

We must not be greedy for gain. We can desire to
prosper and present ourselves before the Lord as hard
workers. We can be visionaries ready to pursue any
great financial idea He may bring our way. But

3

remember, focusing on gain alone is often accompanied by haste, recklessness, and a disregard for what our pursuits might be robbing us of.

๛ Turn ๏

Wisdom calls outside; she utters her voice in the streets: She cries in the chief place of concourse, in the openings of the gates: in the city she utters her words, saying, "How long, you simple ones, will you love simplicity and the scorners delight in their scorning, and fools hate knowledge? Turn at my correction: behold, I will pour out my spirit to you, I will make known my words to you."

Proverbs 1:20-23

Wisdom is calling out to us throughout our days everywhere we go:

'Don't buy that'

'Do your dishes'

'Sit down with your children'

'Make your bed'

'Pay that bill'

'Finish that project'

'Get off the internet'

'Wash that car'

'Get out of this conversation'

We need to hear wisdom speaking to us to have our days ordered by the Lord. If we would turn at wisdom's correction, we would have the Lord's Spirit poured out on to us, hearing more readily the next time.

Since wisdom speaks, we need to listen. When we listen we need to take heed to wisdom's directives. Wisdom is a friend from God giving us good counsel, great principles, and telling us how to prioritize our lives.

Let's obey wisdom and enjoy the fact that, even if we have been foolish, wisdom is speaking and ready to build our lives as God desires them to be built.

❧ Calamity ☙

Because I have called, and you refused; I have stretched out my hand, and no man regarded; But you have disregarded all my counsel, and would have none of my correction: I also will laugh at your calamity; I will mock when your fear comes; When your fear comes as desolation, and your destruction comes as a whirlwind; when distress and anguish comes upon you. Then shall they call upon me, but I will not answer; they shall seek me early, but they shall not find me:

Proverbs 1:24-28

Sometimes we cry out to the Lord for help in situations our own foolishness got us into. We even remember the Lord trying to give us the wise way to do things in the first place. He loves us so much that when we do call out to Him in our afflictions, He hears us and delights in delivering us. In some cases it will be difficult to hear the wise way out. This could be a result of our own stubbornness and refusal to hear in the first place. We must humble ourselves when we get into messes and be quiet before the Lord, that we might receive the wisdom we need to get through such calamity.

When we refuse when He calls, setting His counsel aside, our hearts become calloused. Our ears become less sensitive to His voice. Our paths will be filled with unnecessary distress and aguish. He wants to use these things to show us we have disregarded His counsel. Wisdom will *laugh* at us. We will hear the wisdom we ignored. Wisdom will speak to us through consequences, declaring it should have been obeyed. It will *mock* us because it will be obvious wisdom was right and our foolishness was not.

There will be a time to own our foolishness and we will begin to thirst for wisdom. This will produce in us a great respect for wisdom and disdain for trusting our own hearts. This will bless future decisions and build safe and secure lives.

❧ Safe ☙

For that they hated knowledge, and did not choose the fear of the LORD: They would have none of my counsel: they despised all my correction. Therefore shall they eat of the fruit of their own way, and be filled with their own devices. For the turning away of the simple shall slay them, and the prosperity of fools shall destroy them. But whoever listens with the intent to obey me shall dwell safely, and shall be quiet from fear of evil.

Proverbs 1:29-33

Knowledge and the fear of the Lord are tied together. We should always be seeking things that please the Lord and then we will understand how to live. If we hearken to our OWN understanding we are in danger of making foolish choices.

Oftentimes we eat the fruit of our own ways and blame others or the Lord for such *sour grapes*. We should be thankful when foolish choices turn out horrible, because the prosperity of fools destroys them. This proves God right and turns us back to seeking Him and His ways. The wise choice isn't always the most exciting, but the results of having our steps ordered by the Lord, creates a quiet, safe, lifestyle free from the fear of evil.

When we hearken to and submit our wills to the Lord and His value system, our lives are not filled with sudden, horrible surprises stemming from foolish decisions. We end up in a safe place. We are not dodging ugly consequences brought about by relying on reasoning or choices that are in direct opposition to our Maker's design for our lives and days.

ೞ Seek ೞ

My son, if you will receive my words, and hide my commandments with you; So that you incline your ear to wisdom, and apply your heart to understanding; Yes, if you cry after knowledge, and lift up your voice for understanding; If you seek her as silver, and search for her as for hidden treasures; Then you will understand the fear of the LORD, and find the knowledge of God.

Proverbs 2:1-5

There are a lot of *ifs* in this section. In this proverb eight different exhortations are directly linked to receiving the fear of the Lord and the knowledge of God.

Receive	Apply	Seek
Hide	Cry	Search
Incline	Speak	

Our ears need to be intentionally listening for the Lord. We must passionately pursue the Lord. We are to have a fervency in spirit delighted to discover all He has saved us to experience. It is an act of our wills and we must consciously position ourselves to actively *seek* God — not just *observe* or *mentally assent* to His existence.

God is referring to our ears, hearts, emotions, voices, eyes and postures. We must love Him with all of our hearts, souls, minds and strength. He deserves nothing less. We benefit from a fervent pursuit of the Lord who has pursued us. If we are lazy we will have a sluggish perception of God. If we take the challenge of such a pursuit, we will find ourselves with a bounty of insight and a heightened sense of how mighty and powerful He is. We will be greatly impressed. Our admiration will increase and we will all the more readily yield to Him.

❧ ഇ Plenty ൡ

For the LORD gives wisdom: out of his mouth comes knowledge and understanding. He lays up sound wisdom for the righteous: he is a shield close to them that walk uprightly. He keeps the paths of judgment, and protects the way of his saints. Then will you understand righteousness, and judgment, and equity; yes, every good path.

Proverbs 2:6-9

The Lord has an account filled with wisdom for us. When we approach Him for wisdom we can be confident we are going to the One who He has plenty to give. The Lord tells us in James 1:5, *"But if any of you lacks wisdom, let him ask of God, who gives to all men generously and without reproach, and it will be given to him."* He is guarding the paths of judgment and His standards don't change. He is preserving our paths and wants to lead us in the right way.

When we go to the Lord for His judgment on a matter we will gain understanding. We will learn what is right and fair. We will be instructed on what a good life really is. He is the One who created life. He knows us, loves us, and has the clear-cut wisest choice in every matter.

His mouth gives knowledge and understanding. We hear Him speak in the written Word of God. This is why we should have a consistent time and place of being taught His Word. These disciplines will equip us when a decision demands our attention. We cannot go to the User's Manual only at the time we need guidance and judgment. Being in the *paths* of judgment consistently allows us to be people who gain good judgment *before* we are in a place where judgment must be made.

☙ Deliverance ☞

When wisdom enters into your heart, and knowledge is pleasant to your soul; Discretion shall preserve you, understanding shall keep you: To deliver you from the way of the evil man, from the man that speaks twisted things;

Proverbs 2:10-12

Wisdom must be more than just admired and espoused. Wisdom must enter our hearts and we must delight to do the right things. If we don't really *want* to do things God's way, wisdom *will not* deliver us. A life preserver on display near the pool won't save one who is drowning unless it is received and used by the person who needs it. Unless we receive and use wisdom, we won't benefit from it.

We need to have "discretion": *the ability to assess things based on wisdom versus foolishness.* Discretion wants to show us how to use our time, tongues, money etc. We need to have discretion. It will preserve us and guard us from unnecessary conflict, waste and wounds.

We need to be delivered from people who speak the wrong things. People who teach and deliver philosophies contrary to the Lord are labeled "evil" in this proverb. Do we see them as evil or do we admire educators, politicians, or celebrities who promote the very things Christ died for on Calvary?

When we are people of wisdom we will not be easily seduced or deceived by foolishness masking as true wisdom.

⁊ Twisted Ↄ

Who leave the paths of uprightness, to walk in the
ways of darkness; who rejoice to do evil, and delight in
the twistedness of the wicked; whose ways are
crooked, and they are twisted in their paths:

Proverbs 2:13 – 15

People laugh at evil things in the name of
entertainment. Many reality shows find great joy in
scripting things God calls evil. They script perverse
and bizarre scenarios hoping to draw the greatest
number of viewers.

The paths of uprightness are safe. They can seem
boring at times but are we here for excitement or to
dwell safely?   The Lord says in Jeremiah 32:37b,
"...and I will cause them to dwell safely:" Do we *really*
enjoy crooked paths? We can't enjoy the journey
when we have to keep looking down to be sure we
are on the path. Wisdom will deliver us from this
sort of life so we will dwell safely and enjoy the
journey!

৪০ Retain ০৪

To deliver you from the strange woman, even from the
stranger which flatters with her words; which forsakes
the guide of her youth, and forgets the covenant of her
God. For her house inclines to death, and her paths to
the dead. None that go to her return again, neither take
they hold of the paths of life.

Proverbs 2:16-19

Wisdom and discretion are given to deliver us from the
strange woman. This *strange woman* can be likened to
our fallen nature. We should never use words to gain
someone's favor or get what we want. We are cautioned
about people who place their words in a way to *flatter*.

Men are warned to avoid women who have these
attributes. There are women who use these tactics to
lure men. God wants to deliver men and women from
this type of person – either being this woman or having
her seduce them.

Have you forsaken the guide of your youth? This would
be the Holy Spirit for us as believers today. Have you
been with the Lord so long you really think you can
navigate your own life? Don't be someone who forsakes
or forgets. Rather, *retain and remember*. Stay close to
your guide and ponder the covenant with your God.
Renew your commitment to Him today and look for
His leading in every step.

ঙ Remain ঙ

That you may walk in the way of good men, and keep the paths of the righteous. For the upright shall dwell in the land, and the mature shall remain in it. But the wicked shall be cut off from the earth, and the transgressors shall be rooted out of it.

Proverbs 2:20-22

The Lord desires us to walk in a *good* way. He wants us to have friends and companions who are vessels of His love and faithfulness. He wants us to be challenged by those around us and stirred up to run the race more steadfastly than ever before.

We must be willing to be searched by our God. We should desire to walk in an upright manner. Our life choices are to be built upon the revealed Word of God. This will assure us of a sure-footed life and help us avoid confusion and instability.

No one will get away with anything. We are told in Galatians 6:9, *"Let us not become weary in doing good, for at the proper time we will reap a harvest if we do not give up."* We take our orders from our Creator and Maker. A farmer confidently waits for the harvest, knowing seed is taking root even when he doesn't see anything above ground. We, too, must continue steadfast in making wise choices regardless of what we see, confident we will reap a harvest as well.

ও Guard ন্ত

My son, forget not my law; but let your heart keep my commandments: For length of days, and long life, and peace, shall they add to you.

Proverbs 3:1-2

If the Lord tells us *not* to forget the Law then we are correct in concluding our tendency is *to forget* the Law.

Our hearts are to keep His commandments. This word "keep" means to guard or protect. Do you fight for your time in the Word of God at church or alone with the Lord? Do you protect and guard that time, not allowing opposing forces to come in and steal it away?

Recently, I went to get my wedding ring cleaned. The jeweler noticed a prong had bent and the diamond was about to fall out. What an expensive tragedy that might have been! My diamond is of great value to me. I took the ring off and put it in a safe place until I could get it fixed. This is the type of guarding we should do when it comes to the jewels of His truth. We should review truths we've heard and be careful not to lose jewels we have been given. Think, right now. What is one *jewel* you have received from the Word of God in the last week? Do you remember or is the *prong* a bit loose?

Long life, better days and peace come from His commandments. How foolish we are when we neglect such wonderful benefits by forgetting His Word or treating His commandments so casually.

❧ Mercy ☙

Let not mercy and truth leave you: bind them about your neck; write them upon the table of your heart: So you will find favor and good understanding in the sight of God and man.

Proverbs 3:3-4

Mercy and truth help us in our relationships with God and people. We need to see things as they truly are and choose to have mercy.

Mercy is being able to recognize something as a legitimate short coming and choosing to let it go. You cannot have mercy without truth. These two attributes allow us to experience healthy relationships. We can communicate if we have been offended or sinned against — that is the truth. We can communicate calmly and with the intent of being merciful — that is mercy. These two will help us with our human relationships and please the Lord as well. When God sees our lives He sees everything in truth and yet in His mercy deals with us patiently. He extends acceptance regardless of where we are in the maturing process. Let us have mercy and truth in all of our dealings and see good understanding and favor manifest themselves.

ೕ All ೖ

Trust in the LORD with all your heart; and lean not to your own understanding. In all your ways acknowledge him, and he shall direct your paths.

Proverbs 3:5-6

Answer the following questions aloud based on the verses above:

How much of our hearts should we trust Him with?

Where exactly is this trust supposed to be deposited?

How many of our ways should we consult Him regarding?

Are we allowed to give our own understanding a bit of credibility?

What a wonderful promise! He will order our steps and direct our paths. Our trust, understanding and who we are consulting has everything to do with the direction of our lives. Consider the following questions concerning your life at this moment:

Is there a part of your heart trusting/depending on someone or something else?

Do you trust your analysis more than the God who can do all things?

Are there certain roads in your life you have taken control of and not acknowledged His leading on?

If we seek to understand situations independently of God, we can end up having too much of our own understanding. The more of our own understanding we create, the more tempted we will be to lean on it. Rather than analyzing, let's pray and cast our cares upon Him. Let's ask Him to reveal His will in the situation whether we understand or not. Let's be the sheep that have the security of the Lord Jesus directing our paths by looking to Him to lead us.

Take every thought captive to His obedience today and enjoy Jesus as the Shepherd of your path.

❧ Biased ☙

Be not wise in your own eyes: fear the LORD, and depart from evil. It shall be health to your navel, and marrow to your bones.

Proverbs 3:7-8

When we are told not to be wise in our own eyes, we can be reasonably sure we tend to think we are always right. We must humble ourselves in the presence of the One who has all wisdom. The fear of the Lord will help keep us humble in mind. When we know He alone has the perfect answers, we will be less likely to exalt our own understanding. We will seek Him all the more. Our frames will be strong. We will be able stand against the evil one, get up from falls without serious spiritual injury and be able to support others as well.

We don't have all the knowledge to make judgments that are completely unbiased or include all possible variables. When we remember God is looking upon humanity and sees things with perfect judgment, we will begin seeking Him for His perspective and assessments. We will be slow to speak and quick to listen. We will not be high-minded but position ourselves before Him to receive instruction. We will be confident that He has a perspective that is pure. He is the God who sees all, loves all, and knows all.

Our frames will be much surer and less able to break under the strain of trying to understand and control situations. We will fear the Lord and not be wise in our own eyes. This will allow us to flourish and operate in healthy ways when dealing with people and challenges.

༄ Substance ༅

Honor the LORD with your substance, and with the first fruits of all your increase: So shall your barns be filled with plenty, and your presses shall burst out with new wine.

Proverbs 3:9-10

In what ways could we dishonor the Lord with what we own? How do we use the things He has blessed us with? Do we spend more of our substance on clothing ourselves that *we* might be glorified rather than looking for ways to bring Him honor?

The first fruits means just that — the *first* of everything our lives yield. He deserves the first fruits of our time, money, energy and anything else He has so graciously allowed us to have. Do we give the government the first fruits from our paychecks in taxes, then our bills, and then the leftovers for the Lord? We must be searched and bring by force the first fruits to the Lord however He may direct. There is a great promise here regarding such a priority.

Some people say they cannot give regularly to their local church *because* their barns are barren, but perhaps that is *why* their barns are barren.

ℬ Chastening ℭ

My son, despise not the chastening of the LORD; neither be weary of his correction: For whom the LORD loves he corrects; even as a father the son in whom he delights.

Proverbs 3:11-12

We don't always like discipline, but the Lord loves us enough to straighten us out. When teeth are out of alignment, braces are put on to correct them. Braces hurt and yet produce a transformed smile. His correction can be painful but produces transformed lives.

We see *discipline* is associated with correction. Discipline is a process that should not just include punishment for what is *wrong*, but some sort of measure to bring about the *right* behavior. People need to not only see where they have done the wrong thing, but the standard they are being encouraged to live by. They also need instruction on how to reach the standard.

As children of God, He doesn't just tell us our sins. He instructs us in the things that are right. When we sense the Lord confronting us in a wrongdoing, we need to seek Him as to the correct way He has for us. He shows us the way we *should* go, not just the way we *shouldn't* go.

Let's embrace correction and know He is a good Shepherd leading us into green pastures. He is a Master Potter making us into a beautiful vessel. He is a good Father training us up in the way we *should* go.

ଈ Seeking ଓ

Happy is the man that finds wisdom, and the man that gets understanding. For the merchandise of it is better than the merchandise of silver, and the gain thereof than fine gold. She is more precious than rubies: and all the things you can desire are not to be compared to her. Length of days is in her right hand; and in her left hand riches and honor. Her ways are ways of pleasantness, and all her paths are peace. She is a tree of life to them that lay hold upon her: and happy is every one that retains her.

Proverbs 3:13-18

Wisdom and understanding must be found and received. We do not look *within* we look *up*. Just like we might enjoy looking for the best deal in a department store, on the car lot, or in a thrift store, we must look eagerly for the wise way of handling a matter. This will give us understanding the Lord would want us to have.

Wisdom, choices made by the Lord's standards, makes a pleasant life and peaceful rewards. If we foolishly squander our time instead of doing those things we should do, we usually end up with an unpleasant attitude and anything *but* a peaceful household. We need to wisely handle our time. If we choose to forsake wisdom, our journeys are usually quite tumultuous and unpleasant. We need to retain wisdom and continue building our homes, businesses, and relationships not upon what we *want* to do, but upon wisdom's counsel and leading.

❧ Establishes ☙

The LORD by wisdom has founded the earth; by understanding has he established the heavens. By his knowledge the depths are broken up, and the clouds drop down the dew.

Proverbs 3:19-20

The Lord used wisdom to create the earth with an incredible balance in nature, seasons, and ecosystems. We can take comfort in knowing wisdom will bring about a flow in our lives that makes for refreshing, balanced living.

Is it wise to drive through that fast food restaurant when there is food at home? Would it be wise to try and make a large meal when we have a commitment in 45 minutes? Would it be wise to sleep that extra 30 minutes and forsake our time with the Lord? Is it wise to sit down and watch that movie when the dishes are piled up?

As much as the Lord used wisdom to order the earth, we need wisdom to order our lives. He has promised to give us wisdom so that our lives are balanced and in order.

ಐ Sleep ೞ

*My son, let not them depart from your eyes: keep sound
wisdom and discretion: So shall they be life to your soul,
and grace to your neck. Then will you walk in your way
safely, and your foot shall not stumble. When you lie
down, you will not be afraid: yes, you will lie down, and
your sleep shall be sweet.*

Proverbs 3:21-24

We must treasure God's principles and not let them go
to the wayside. Wisdom causes us to walk safely and
avoid unnecessary detours. Many troubles come from
foolish decisions. Sometimes they are sinful decisions
and other times they are just not the wisest choices.

Don't we want to lie down without worrying about the
debt we were never to accumulate in the first place?
Don't we want to have sweet sleep because we aren't so
behind because we worked rather than played? Let's
not fall back into foolish patterns. Perhaps the anxiety
preventing us from falling asleep is rooted in foolish
decisions. May we enjoy the sweet sleep that comes
from lives built with wisdom.

❧ Confidence ☙

Be not afraid of sudden fear, neither of the desolation of the wicked, when it comes. For the LORD shall be your confidence, and shall keep your foot from being taken.

Proverbs 3:25-26

What a sweet promise for us! The Lord will be our confidence. He shall keep our feet from being taken. He looks out for us and His counsels are to be relied upon. The Lord *Himself* is to be our confidence.

When we take counsel He gives us and implement it into our decisions, values, and priorities, we create lives that are built according to code. We won't have to be afraid of sudden fear. We are not operating on impulse, in deception or without regard to the truths that God has woven into His creation. As we guard wisdom, He guards us.

❧ Relationships ☙

Withhold not good from them to whom it is due, when it is in the power of your hand to do it. Say not to your neighbor, Go, and come again, and tomorrow I will give; when you have it by you. Devise not evil against your neighbor, seeing he dwells securely by you. Do not strive with a man without a good reason, if he has done you no harm.

Proverbs 3:27-30

If we can pay someone back money we owe them, we should. We must reject any temptation to use the money on other things when it is owed to someone. If we owe money for a bill and we can pay it, we must do this first before buying what we want. If it is within our power to help someone we must remain ready and willing to do good.

We must be careful to get along with those who are around us. Our neighbors, co-workers, roommates, and those who work alongside us in ministry, should feel safe from plotting or plans to punish or make life miserable for them. We must remember that the Lord is the Judge of the living and He will render to a man what discipline he needs. We must seek to honor the Lord with our treatment and thoughts toward others.

ᙦ Glorious ᙦ

*Do not envy the oppressor, and choose none of his ways.
For the twisted is an abomination to the LORD: but his
secret is with the righteous. The curse of the LORD is in
the house of the wicked: but he blesses the habitation of
the just. Surely he scorns the scorners: but he gives grace
to the lowly. The wise shall inherit glory: but shame shall
be the promotion of fools.*

Proverbs 3:31-35

We can look at others and wish we had what they had.
The problem is we don't see *all* they have. They might
have the nice house and nice cars but they also may
have the nice child-support payments, tax-liens against
that nice house, bitterness that makes them angry at
the world, and few faithful friends in their lives.

Our homes will be blessed as we do those things that
are right. We should make our children's training a
priority over our own careers or education. We need to
make our mates the objects of our respect and
affection. We are to realize that life is not defined by
an abundance of possessions. When we do these things
we will have blessed habitations.

The Lord wants our habitations blessed. When we
make wise choices according to God's counsel, our
homes will be blessed. We will have glorious lives and
the trials we face will not be a direct result of our own
foolish choices. We will avoid unnecessary problems.
Wisdom will give us a glorious life but foolishness will
bring shame.

ॐ **Fathers** ৪৪

Hear, you children, the instruction of a father, and attend to know understanding. For I give you good doctrine, do not forsake my law. For I was my father's son, tender and only beloved in the sight of my mother. He taught me also, and said to me, Let your heart retain my words: keep my commandments, and live.

Proverbs 4:1-4

Even if your own father is not alive or able to instruct you in righteousness, the proverbs themselves are here to *father* you and give you good doctrine.

"Doctrine" means *something received* or *learning*. The wisdom the Lord is teaching us within the Word is that which we can receive, becomes part of who we are and why we do what we do.

As we retain, or grasp, what wisdom is telling us to do, we will experience life as the Lord intended. Our Heavenly Father will fill our days with life. We will no longer merely exist, we will truly live.

ঙ Lists ଓ

Get wisdom, get understanding: forget it not; neither decline from the words of my mouth. Forsake her not, and she shall protect you: love her, and she shall guard you. Wisdom is the most important thing to get first; therefore get wisdom: and with all your getting get understanding.

Proverbs 4:5-7

If the Lord tells us to get wisdom we must *not* have it naturally. It isn't until we realize this, that we will humble ourselves and *ask* Him for it. If we face frustrating situations we need wisdom. We need to *go and get it.*

When you and I get that wisdom we must not forsake it. We must *continue* in those things that the Lord has instructed us to do. This results in our lives being preserved. We will not succumb to the decay that trials and pressures try to bring into our lives.

We always have a list of things we either *need* or *want.* We are instructed to get wisdom and understanding above everything — first on the shopping list, first on the wish list, first on the errand list — *Get Wisdom and Understanding!*

❧ Question ☙

Exalt her, and she shall promote you: she shall bring you to honor, when you embrace her. She shall give to your head an ornament of grace: a crown of glory shall she deliver to you.

Proverbs 4:8-9

Wisdom is to be esteemed, admired and sought out in every decision we make. Wisdom will help us rise in authority over foolish responses that seek to rule our lives. A good question when making choices is, *"Is this wise or is this foolish/fleshly?"* We can use the wisdom test given in James 3:17 to evaluate our decisions:

A Test for Wisdom

- Is it pure or is there any hint of deception or selfish motives?
- Is there anything sinful or evil in it?
- Is it clouded with hidden agendas?
- Is it peaceable or will it cause unnecessary conflict or division?
- Is it gentle or are am I trying to force an issue?
- Is it easy to be entreated or am I forcing myself to do it?
- Is there any judgment associated with it or is it full of mercy and not linked to some sort of retribution or punishment?
- Could good results abound as a result of this choice?
- Is the answer biased or based on preconceived ideas of what I really want to do or without partiality?

- Is it in direct conflict with what I know the Lord has already told me to do in His Word or otherwise?

If you run a decision by these criteria it should help you recognize if it is a wise or foolish choice.

❧ Follow ❦

Hear, O my son, and receive my sayings; and the years of your life shall be many. I have taught you in the way of wisdom; I have led you in right paths. When you go, your steps shall not be restricted; and when you run, you will not stumble.

Proverbs 4:10-12

We need to hear *and* receive what the Lord tells us. A good prayer to pray before we enter into the Word is that we would *receive* His Word. When His truths become part of our identity we begin to think like the Lord — with wisdom that is tested and proven.

The Lord has the right paths designed to support and direct us to the destinations He has for us. He leads us in these paths. He is right in front of us. More than focusing on the path, we should focus on the Leader.

❧ Stay Away ☙

Take firm hold of instruction; do not let her go: keep her; for she is your life. Enter not into the path of the wicked, and go not in the way of evil men. Avoid it, pass not by it, turn from it, and pass away. For they sleep not, except they have done mischief; and their sleep is taken away, unless they cause some to fall. For they eat the bread of wickedness, and drink the wine of violence.

Proverbs 4:13-17

We tend to let go of basic instructions. We must ask the Lord to weave His truth into the fabric of our lives. We must not let it go. It must become a part of our identities and courses of life.

He warns us not to even take a *step* in the path of the wicked. This is a warning about *where* we go not just the people that are there. We are to avoid it, not pass by it, turn from it and not go near it. The Lord knows that if we are in the wrong place we can end up with the wrong people. Then we might end up doing wrong things. We could end up with unnecessary pain and destruction brought on by being in the wrong place.

Because He loves us He warns us. Let's embrace Him by embracing His warnings.

ଚ Brighter ଓ

But the path of the just is as the shining light, that shines more and more to the perfect day. The way of the wicked is as darkness: they do not even know what they stumble over when they stumble.

Proverbs 4:18-19

Sometimes we are sinned against by an unbeliever or see choices in their life that surprise us. We might wonder how they couldn't see that these decisions are foolish, sinful or destructive. The path of the wicked is covered in darkness. People who have yet to surrender to Christ are stumbling over things they cannot see. We need to have and extend mercy on those in darkness. The best thing we can do is lead a person to the light. It is not try to explain all that they are stumbling over. When people come to the Light, He will reveal what they need to see.

Jesus is the Light of the world. As His disciples, we should be seeing things more clearly the longer we have been following Him. There is little excuse for us to make hasty decisions when we are given light to carefully evaluate our paths. Every time we make righteous decisions, we will see more clearly. Our paths will shine brighter and brighter, proving God truly has no darkness in Him at all.

❧ Life ☙

My son, attend to my words; incline your ear to my sayings. Let them not depart from your eyes; keep them in the midst of your heart. For they are life to those that find them, and health to all their flesh.

Proverbs 4:20-22

We need to attend to the Lord's Words and bow down our understanding to all He has to say. Being exposed to His truth should be a discipline in our lives. The scriptures teach us that we should, "... *give attendance to reading...*" (1 Tim 4:13). Apart from in-depth bible study, reading His Word will expose us to healthy truths.

His Words will be health to our flesh. In the book of Proverbs there are many practical commands about sleep, work, eating, finances and our words. Forgiveness releases us of stresses that bear hard on our hearts and circulatory systems. Trust, rather than anxiety, will guard our respiratory systems and blood pressure. His Words *are* life to us and health to all our flesh.

❧ Hearts ❧

Keep your heart with all diligence; for out of it are the issues of life. Put away from you a twisted mouth, and perverse lips put far from you. Let your eyes look right on, and let your eyelids look straight before you.
Ponder the path of your feet, and let all your ways be established. Turn not to the right hand nor to the left: remove your foot from evil.

Proverbs 4:23-27

God gives us instructions for the courses of our lives. They start with our hearts and end with our feet.

The Lord knows that our paths begin with *our hearts*. What do we cherish and value? What are our meditations, goals and affections? Do they line up with the Lord's heart for us and His purpose for our lives? We are exhorted to keep our hearts with *all* diligence. Our hearts are to be consistently searched by our Maker.

How do we keep our hearts this way? Hebrews 4:12 tells us the Word of God *"... is quick, and powerful, and sharper than any two-edged sword...and is a discerner of the thoughts and intents of the heart."* Listening to the Word of God with a vulnerability will keep us challenged, rebuked and corrected.

Our thoughts should be quieted in order to hear the Holy Spirit point something out that is good or wrong in our hearts. The Lord tells us in Romans 8:26-27, *"Likewise the Spirit also helps infirmities: ...And he that searches the hearts knows what is the mind of the Spirit..."*

The tongue has so much power. We must ask the Lord to put a guard over our mouths and have purposed words that build up, not tear down. Our mouths must not be allowed to ramble on with self-pity, self-exaltation, self-anything. Our mouths should declare His praises and point others to Him.

Then we have *the eyes* related to *our feet*. What are we watching or reading? Where is our focus? *"My eyes are ever toward the LORD; for he shall pluck my feet out of the net."* (Ps 25:15) Who are we looking to in order that our needs are met?

Our hearts, tongues, eyes and feet are keys to experiencing the lives our Lord has for us. Our hearts are to be searched. Our tongues need to be under His control. Our eyes need to look to the Lord, causing our feet to follow.

ಐ Bow ೞ

My son, attend to my wisdom, and bow your ear to
my understanding: That you may regard discretion,
and that your lips may keep knowledge.

Proverbs 5:1-2

Wisdom is given to the one who is attentive. If we
go through life haphazardly making decisions, our
lives will not be built with wisdom. As we go
through our days, we must remain attentive to
wisdom's voice and be willing to stop something
midstream if wisdom tells us to.

In order to understand life, relationships, finances
etc., we must bow *down* our ears. We are to listen
with a humble state of mind. We should be open to
throwing out preconceived ideas, receiving
instruction from our Maker.

If we want our lips to speak wisdom, we must have
this sort of attentive humility in approaching our
lives.

❧ Unfaithfulness ❧

For the lips of a strange woman drop as a honeycomb, and her mouth is smoother than oil: But her end is bitter as wormwood, sharp as a two-edged sword. Her feet go down to death; her steps take hold on hell. Lest you should ponder the path of life, her ways are unstable, that you cannot know them. Hear me now therefore, O you children, and depart not from the words of my mouth. Remove your way far from her, and do not come near the door of her house: or else you will give your honor to others, and your years to the cruel: this will result in strangers be filled with your wealth; and your labors be in the house of a stranger; And you mourn at the last, when your flesh and your body are consumed, And say, How have I hated instruction, and my heart despised correction; And have not obeyed the voice of my teachers, nor inclined mine ear to them that instructed me!

Proverbs 5:3-13

A *strange woman* refers to someone we are not to be bonded with. Our marriage relationship is with the Lamb of God and His Lordship in our lives. When we listen to other voices that try to woo us into investing our time and obedience to them, our stories have a bitter ending and our honor is given to others.

These *voices* are smooth and sometimes we don't even recognize we are being courted by some sin or worthless pursuit. We suddenly wake up and realize that we hated instruction and despised correction.

It is also a warning to a man who would be tempted to bond with a woman other than his wife. This can be from any source, from a pornographic medium to an actual face-to-face encounter with a woman in the flesh. A man will lose all he has if he allows a strange woman to entice him. What he first thought was so ravishing will become nothing but ruins.

We must listen to the Lord's words and remove ourselves from these paths. We are not to ponder the paths that our Lord has asked us not to travel. These paths are unsteady and the rules are always changing. We must love correction and take heed to warnings. Our Heavenly Father is giving us warnings to lead us away from unnecessary destruction into a life that is filled with goodness and stability.

WISHING YOU A VERY
MERRY CHRISTMAS

with love

Robert, Vero & Desi
2018 Jer. 29:11

✌ Ravished ☙

*I was almost in all evil in the midst of the
congregation and assembly. Drink waters out of your
own cistern, and running waters out of your own well.
Let your fountains be dispersed abroad, and rivers of
waters in the streets. Let them be only your own, and
not strangers' with you. Let your fountain be blessed:
and rejoice with the wife of your youth. Let her be as
the loving hind and pleasant roe; let her breasts
satisfy you at all times; and be ravished always with
her love. And why will you, my son, be ravished with a
strange woman, and embrace the bosom of a
stranger? For the ways of man are before the eyes of
the LORD, and he ponders all his goings. His own
iniquities shall take the wicked himself, and he shall
be bound and restricted with the cords of his sins. He
shall die without instruction; and in the greatness of
his foolishness he shall go astray.*

Proverbs 5:14-23

Marriage is special. The Lord wants a man and
woman to experience a level of commitment that
reflects His commitment to us — His bride. He
wants marriages to be full of refreshment,
nourishment, safety, and contentment.

A wife can look at these verses and learn that they
need to be available to their husbands at all times
for their satisfaction. A wife should live in such a
way that she is described as loving and pleasant. A
wife is to make her husband her highest priority
next to the Lord. She should seek to bless him and
contribute all she can to the quality of his life. A wife
can pray that her husband will always be ravished
with her love. The word "ravished" can be translated
as "intoxicated". A wife's love is to intoxicate her

husband so he is less likely to fell the cruel, destructive arrows of his adversary.

A husband is to rejoice with the wife of his youth. She should be his priority. He should seek to make her feel safe and secure in his love. He is to be ravished with her love, expressing his commitment and attraction to her.

It is important for us to know the intimacy between a man and woman in marriage has been designed by God and should be treated with great care and investment. If we are married, we must never just exist in it. Let's invest in and appreciate it.

ঙ Debt ০৩

My son, if you have gotten into a financial commitment on behalf of a friend, if you have entered into a contract with a stranger, You are snared with the words of your mouth, you are taken with the words of your mouth. Do this now, my son, and deliver yourself, when you are come into the hand of your friend; go, humble yourself, and try to resolve this with your friend. Do not go to sleep. Deliver yourself as a deer from the hand of the hunter, and as a bird from the hand of those that hunt birds.

Proverbs 6:1-5

It is not wise to enter into financial commitments hastily. If we realize we may have made a mistake, we should seek to be released from the commitment if possible. If we lose the money, we lose it. If we can pay quickly and be released of such dealings, let's pay it. We are not to be co-signers for others unless we are prepared to pay the debt. If someone is unable to repay us, we should release them of the debt or come up with a doable repayment plan. If we casually co-sign but are unprepared if our friends fail to pay, it can place friendships under great strain.

If we are in great debt, we shouldn't procrastinate allowing interest to accumulate. Let's wake up! Let's make a plan and stick to it! We will be as birds delivered from traps and fly financially free again.

๛ Ants ๏

Go to the ant, you sluggard; consider her ways, and be wise: Which having no guide, overseer, or ruler, provides her meat in the summer, and gathers her food in the harvest. How long will you sleep, O sluggard? When will you arise out of your sleep? Yet a little sleep, a little slumber, a little folding of the hands to sleep: So shall your poverty come as one that wanders from town to town, and your lack as an armed man.

Proverbs 6:6-11

In the summertime I do not enjoy housework! Hot water, vacuums, folding hot laundry out of the dryer, and cooking are just not appealing when the weather tells you to sit down and drink lemonade. I always think it is strange that during the warmest summer months we have an ant problem. It's almost like the Lord knows I need to go to the ant, consider her ways and be wise. He brings these ants to me in order to wake me up from my sluggish summer ways and look well to the ways of my household. These precious, seemingly insignificant creatures are here partly to teach us lazy humans a thing or two.

In the summer, ants look for water and they are militant about it. One summer day, I went into my laundry closet and there was an organized line of these tiny creatures going up the wall. They climbed up to the shelf, up the iron and into the small opening where I put water in for steam pressing. Talk about diligence! They found water in the laundry closet! They also reminded me that ironing was necessary in the heat of summer as well as the cozy times of winter!

These ants are diligent without someone checking up on them. As employees, homemakers or people who have a task to do, we need to know we are working for the Lord. We should work as diligently when someone is watching, as well as when no one is watching. The Lord rewards the diligent and He rewards in public that which is done in secret.

❧ Division ☙

A naughty person, a wicked man, walks with a twisted mouth. He winks with his eyes, he speaks with his feet, he teaches with his fingers; Twistedness is in his heart, he devises mischief continually; he plants seeds that breed division. Therefore shall his calamity come suddenly; suddenly shall he be broken without remedy.

Proverbs 6:12-15

People are selling everything from self-pity to impulsive, sinful adventures. They are people who are lying and not speaking the clear truth. They speak with an element of truth and yet something isn't quite right. These people plant seeds in the hearts of men and women that cause contention and division. They might come through the media, academic thought or family members. We must remove ourselves from these people and pray that the Lord will expose, deal with and cause them to walk uprightly.

We must make sure we avoid being these types of people. Are we upright and dealing honestly? We must be careful about devising plans that are not pleasing to the Lord. We must not have fantasies or imaginations that God defines as evil.

We must *never* knowingly contribute to division between people. We must *not* love drama. We are to be peacemakers and seek to keep unity as much as possible, with the exception of that which might divide because of convictions or calling.

The Lord doesn't want us to participate in schemes and conversations that put people in certain camps. If we are people who plant seeds of division, calamity will come. Suddenly. Let's pursue peace and recognize those who are busybodies, avoiding or confronting them so we partner with the Lord, walking in the light.

ꙮ Abominations ꙮ

These six things the LORD hates: yes, seven are an abomination to him: A proud look, a lying tongue, and hands that shed innocent blood, a heart that devises wicked imaginations, feet that are swift in running to mischief, a false witness who speaks lies, and he who cultivates division among brethren.

Proverbs 6:16-19

If we love someone we will avoid doing anything that bothers them. If we know they hate a certain type of food, we will not prepare that food for their dinner. If we love the Lord it is good to know what He hates. Here we see a list of seven things that our Lord   hates.

A Proud Look: In Isaiah 2:11 we read, *"The arrogant looks of man shall be humbled, and the haughtiness of men shall be bowed down, and the LORD alone shall be exalted in that day."* Our haughtiness can often be seen by our facial expressions. Some of us have had an opportunity to see ourselves on a video when the Holy Spirit was not controlling us. *What a shock!* We are to humble our hearts and take special care to notice if we roll our eyes, look up out of frustration or smirk.

A Lying Tongue: The Lord hates lies. He is the truth. These are relationship killers. They interrupt our fellowship with the Lord and with each other. We need the Spirit of Truth to flow through us and point out any sort of lie, deceit, and misrepresentation of facts. When we label others with our words, we are not speaking the truth and are, in fact, lying. We need to be sure that the words of our mouths and the meditations of our hearts are acceptable in the sight of God, our strength and our redeemer.

Hands that Shed Innocent Blood: In our culture this could include gang killings, murders brought about through greed or anger and the murder of unborn children. We need to know God hates it when innocent people are murdered. We must realize that anyone who is the victim of murder is on the Lord's heart and it grieves Him every time it happens.

A Heart that Devises Wicked Imaginations: The Lord doesn't want us using our imaginations and thoughts to plan evil things. He is against those who gather together to reassure each other that what they are doing is right when, in fact, God says it is wrong. We are not to rehearse what we wish we could say or do to someone in retaliation. We are not to explore sinful fantasies or ideas that fly in the face of God's standards.

Feet that are Swift in Running to Mischief: Along with being against the planning of evil things is the Lord's hatred for those who are quick to run to mischief. We must be cautious about impulsive decisions or getting caught up in a mob mentality that entices us to run in directions that God says are not good.

A False Witness who Speaks Lies: God's Spirit is called the Spirit of Truth. The father of lies is Satan. We are not to be exaggerators, liars or those who distort facts for our advantage. If we have lied or find ourselves in the midst of a lie, we need to go back and set things right demonstrating that we hate what God hates.

He who Stirs up Division among Brothers: To gossip, malign or plant negative thoughts in someone toward someone else is something God does not like — He hates it! He desires unity and good relationships for His people. Just like an earthly parent loves to see her or his children get along and be friends, our Heavenly Father declares that unity is good and pleasant. If we are someone who loves drama and relishes in starting conflict, we are doing something the Lord hates.

Let's ask God to give us His hatred for these things. His Spirit will point out where we may be emulating or in danger of going toward these behaviors. Remember, we should love what He loves and hates what He hates. He only hates those things because He loves *us*.

ഇ Parents ‍ഇ

*My son, keep your father's commandment, and do not
let go of the law of your mother: Bind them
continually upon your heart, and tie them about your
neck. When you go, it shall lead you; when you sleep,
it shall keep you; and when you awake, it shall talk
with you. For the commandment is a lamp; and the
law is light; and reproofs of instruction are the way of
life:*

Proverbs 6:20-23

Even if we were raised by parents who were not
following Christ, the Lord used them in authority
over our lives. Even when we are older, we can still
draw on many of the things that they imparted to
us. Whether it's making our beds, being on time,
saying "please" or "thank you", or financial wisdom,
we need to take heed to the wisdom we have learned
from our parents. We must test it against the Word
of God and if it agrees, we should keep and not
forsake what we've been taught. These instructions
will contribute to restful sleep and guide us when we
are awake.

Commandments are good. They let us know what to
do and what not to do. We need to embrace
authority and trust that the Lord is using commands
given to us for our good.

The scriptures teach us: *"....that, first of all,
supplications, prayers, intercessions, and giving of
thanks, be made for all men; For kings, and for all
that are in authority; that we may lead a quiet and
peaceable life in all godliness and honesty."* (1 Tim
2:1-2)

We are commanded to pray, intercede, and give
thanks for authority that is currently over us, as well

as authority that ruled us in the past. So many people live in the present blaming past authority for their unrighteous treatment. We need to stop and thank the Lord for the mistakes our parents might have made. The areas where they might have fallen short can serve as examples that we might avoid in our lives. We must pray, consciously pray, for those in authority over us; our landlords, mates, parents, governing officials, teachers, pastors, church leaders, law enforcement personnel, managers and any others who have influence and authority over our lives. All who are in authority need our prayers and we should thank the Lord for them.

When we stop, pray, and give thanks, we resist the temptation to blame or resist authority. We will accept reproof as a way of life for our good and training.

Perhaps you could stop now, pray, and give thanks for your mom and dad and ask the Lord to show you what He would have you remember and retain from their instruction.

ஐ Adultery ௸

To keep you from the evil woman, from the flattery of the tongue of a strange woman.

Lust not after her beauty in your heart; neither let her take you with her eyelids. For by means of a loose woman a man is brought to a piece of bread: and the adulteress will hunt for the precious life. Can a man take fire in his bosom, and his clothes not be burned? Can one go upon hot coals, and his feet not be burned? So he that goes in to his neighbor's wife; whosoever touches her shall not be innocent.

Proverbs 6:24-29

Sexual sin is lurking at the door of your life. You cannot even entertain the thought of an adulterous relationship as something to be toyed with. We see adultery likened to hot coals. Hot coals burn, singe and scar. No one will get away with this sin. The Lord promises that. Children suffer and mates carry wounds of betrayal for years. If either adulterer is a believer, the gospel is disgraced among a world that so needs to be drawn to its truth and beauty.

If you find yourself attracted to someone who is married to another or is not married to you, pause and bring it before the Lord. Thank the Lord for creating this person and all of the wonderful qualities He has put in him or her. Then give God thanks for *their* marriage, future or children. Move on and thank the Lord for *your* mate, children and home. Ask the Lord to protect you from the deception of adultery or having your heart or eyes go toward this person.

If you have lusted after this person, confess it as sin and ask for cleansing and renewal of your affections and thought life. Do not panic! Trust that in your confession you will be walking in the light. His Spirit will search you and convict you of any compromises within. If you are really overtaken by a fixation on the person, find a trusted spiritual leader and get someone to pray with and hold you accountable for your wandering heart.

Take *every* thought captive to the Lord's obedience and ask Him to show you how to cooperate with His fight for your covenant relationship. Enjoy your life. Live your married or single life to its fullest. Invest everything to guard marriages from even the slightest smoldering coal of this horrific sin.

ೞ Restore ೲ

Men do not despise a thief, if he steals to satisfy his soul when he is hungry; but if he is found, he needs to restore seven times the amount he took; he shall give all the substance of his house.

Proverbs 6:30-31

People understand when others steal for survival. It is not the right thing to do, but we can understand and not be so personally victimized if this were the reason it was done. Restitution and interest on what was taken is still due. We can have compassion when someone is tempted but it still is wrong and needs to be paid back.

If you have taken anything that doesn't belong to you, you must seek to make restitution. Have you borrowed something and lost it? Did you break something that belongs to someone else? Bountifully restore it.

ᏝᎧ Destruction ᏜᎧ

But whoever commits adultery with a woman lacks
understanding: he that does it destroys his own soul.
A wound and dishonor shall he get; and his reproach
shall not be wiped away. For jealousy is the rage of a
man: therefore he will not spare in the day of
vengeance. He will not regard any ransom; neither
will he rest content, though you give many gifts.

Proverbs 6:32-35

Committing adultery cannot be corrected by buying
the injured one a nicer car, perfume or new home.
Oh, for a fleeting moment of passion, a lifetime is
dishonored.

An adulterous woman has a spouse. Her spouse's
jealousy will not be appeased. If we entertain the
thought of an adulterous relationship we must
remember that we are going to enter into a
relationship with that person's mate as well. Not
only do you enter into a relationship with your
lover, but you now have a relationship with their
mate — a relationship of rage, vengeance and
conflict. An adulterous relationship will usher
innumerable losses, conflicts and griefs.

❧ Treasure ☙

My son, keep my words, and lay up my commandments with you. Keep my commandments, and live; and my law as the apple of your eye. Bind them upon your fingers, write them upon the table of your heart. Say to wisdom, you are my sister; and call understanding your relative: That they may keep you from the strange woman, from the stranger which flatters with her words.

Proverbs 7:1-5

We are to take the words the Lord has for us and save them up *within* us. We are to keep and regard them as precious and valuable. We are to write them down and cherish them as part of our very beings. His Word is to be deposited into the account of our identities and the dividends are sure and full of life.

You are treasuring the Word of God by looking at it now. That is great. Take it with you and gaze into the words you read today.

A newly engaged girl gazes at the diamond on her finger, enjoying every facet and display of its beauty and all it represents. Let's take the words He has for us and admire them in the light of His love. Let's keep them as the apple of our eyes and esteem them more authoritative than the "experts" of this world.

In order to enjoy the book of Proverbs, we have to believe wisdom is a good thing and needed. Wisdom should be considered to be a close relative. There should be a family resemblance. Understanding and wisdom are to be associated with us. They are to live among our choices.

Wisdom and understanding will protect us from the strange woman who flatters with her words. A strange woman can be anything that tries to lure us away from sincere devotion to Christ. Wisdom and understanding will help us make choices and priorities that free us up to hear our Good Shepherd's voice. Wisdom and understanding will protect us from following pursuits that result in unfamiliar love, its dangers and damaging repercussions.

๏ Discern ๏

For at the window of my house I looked through my window, and observing among the simple ones, I discerned among the youths, a young man void of understanding, passing through the street near her corner; and he went the way to her house, in the twilight, in the evening, in the black and dark night:

Proverbs 7:6-9

The word "simple" in the Word of God means void of understanding. We must not be *simple* people. We ought to be people who desire to understand the heart of God. The Lord would have us be prudent — able to assess a situation and make choices led by the Lord's wisdom. If we remain simple and do not grow in wisdom we might, like this young man, walk too close to compromise and the traps our adversary has set for us.

ಬ Modesty ಲ

And, behold, there met him a woman with prostitute's clothing, and cunning of heart. (She is loud and stubborn; her feet abide not in her house: Now is she without, now in the streets, and lies in wait at every corner.)

Proverbs 7:10-12

The woman described in this proverb dressed immodestly. When I was a young single Christian I was frustrated because it seemed that all of the godly guys were never interested in me. The guys in my church who only wanted one thing would approach me. I came before the Lord and asked Him about this matter. He led me to a book that was written by my pastor. The book explained that you catch whatever fish you bait your hook for. I was reminded that if I looked like I was carnal, others would perceive me as this. Although the Lord does truly look on the heart, we must realize *"...man looks on the outward appearance."* (1 Sam 16:7)

Modesty is always in vogue among Christian ladies, single and married. A Christian guy friend of mine in college told me to use John the Baptist's motto as a guideline. *"He must increase, but I must decrease."* (John 3:30) When we are at the beach on a hot August day and we wear a long-sleeved turtleneck and sweats we will draw attention to our bodies. If a woman shows up in modest shorts and a t-shirt at a wedding people will look at her.

One thing a woman can do is take time to seek the Lord on His standards for her wardrobe. He will help her choose the best options based on her shape, culture and frame. Women could go to their closets and dressers and lay each item of clothing out and ask Him what He says about it.

Men, you might be initially attracted to the woman who dresses in an enticing way, but might not be the woman the Lord has for you. A woman who dresses this way, does not appear to be ready for a relationship that honors God. She may not be a woman who fears the Lord and could lead you in a pathway of destruction.

She is also credited with being *loud* and *stubborn*. *Loud* speaks of a woman who draws attention to herself in word and action. Her presence intrudes on those who approach her. A woman should resist the temptation to speak all her mind, to demand her way and be the center of attention. This is not the way of a woman who wants to please her Lord. This loudness has to do with clamor, rage and moaning. A woman should ask herself, *"Do I complain and seek my own interests above others? Do I have to be heard or I will insist others listen to me?"* Unlike this woman, a Christian woman has a quietness of heart allowing her to take back seat to His presence and others' interests.

She is also described as *stubborn*. The same Hebrew word used in this proverb is also used in Psalm 78:8:

"And might not be as their fathers, a stubborn and rebellious generation; a generation that set not their heart aright, and whose spirit was not steadfast with God."

Stubbornness is associated with an arrogant heart and a spirit that is not steadfast with God. Women of Christ must be sure to have their hearts open and searched by His Spirit and Word.

A man needs to evaluate if the woman he is pursuing is a strong-willed, stubborn woman not open to correction. She will make mistakes, but is she a woman who is seeking to have God transform her and take her from glory to glory?

This woman *is found out in the streets*. Our culture tries to get women away from the home. Women must have good reasons to leave their homes. This woman was wandering without purpose. Because of that, she entered into a dangerous place of flirting with sin. Women don't need to *hang out* at the mall or *hang out* at church. They should go there with a reason. This will protect her from being in the wrong place at the wrong time.

❧ Flattering ❧

So she caught him, and kissed him, and with an impudent face said to him, I have peace offerings with me; this day have I paid my vows. Therefore I came forth to meet you, diligently to seek your face, and I have found you. I have decked my bed with coverings of tapestry, with carved works, with fine linen of Egypt. I have perfumed my bed with myrrh, aloes, and cinnamon. Come, let us take our fill of love until the morning: let us solace ourselves with loves. For the good man is not at home, he is gone on a long journey: He has taken a bag of money with him, and will come home at the day appointed. With her much flattering speech she caused him to yield, with the flattering of her lips she forced him.

Proverbs 7:13-21

A wicked woman uses bait to catch a man. The woman of God is not to do so. She waits upon the Lord and surrenders her desires to her God. She looks to Him for her steps to be ordered.

This woman lies to the man and says she diligently sought him. We know from the context that she happened to be in the street looking for any fellow to walk by. A godly woman speaks the truth. A woman who gains attention through flattery or deceit has partnered with the father of lies. She gives him permission to destroy lives through her. Men under her persuasion are fed a pack of lies. Through the lies they are enticed, caught up in the moment and ignore the long term consequences of yielding to her.

Don't believe every voice that speaks, especially when it appeals to the moment and senses. It is so important to assess based on wisdom and not the traps that might be baited with just the right words.

We all have tremendous influence with our speech. May our lips speak wisdom and give encouragement to others. May our lips never cause people to yield to sin or compromise.

❧ Wounds ❧

He goes after her straightway, as an ox goes to the
slaughter, or as a fool to the correction of the stocks;
Till a dart strike through his liver; as a bird hastes to
the snare, and knows not that it is for his life.
Hearken to me now therefore, O you children, and
attend to the words of my mouth. Let not your heart
decline to her ways, go not astray in her paths. For
she has cast down many wounded: yes, many strong
men have been slain by her. Her house is the way to
hell, going down to the chambers of death.

Proverbs 7:22-27

Sexual adventures make promises but are usually short-lived and devastating. Sexual sin is a snare and wants to take lives — lives that would have been blessed.

God's words are to be hearkened to and His warnings taken seriously. Going down the road of sexual perversion or compromise causes hearts to decline. The path of sexual sin takes people *down.* Our God tells people to hearken to Him *now.*

O Lord, deliver us from the lusts of the eyes and the lusts of the flesh.

❧ Listening ☙

*Doesn't wisdom cry and understanding put forth her
voice? She stands in the top of high places, by the way
in the places of the paths. She cries at the gates, at
the entry of the city, at the coming in at the doors. To
you, O men, I call; and my voice is to the sons of man.
O you simple-minded, understand wisdom: and, you
fools, be of an understanding heart. Hear; for I will
speak of excellent things; and the opening of my lips
shall be right things.*

Proverbs 8:1-6

Wisdom — God's way of handling things — is
speaking to us in every situation. If we are quiet
enough and slow to react, we will hear wisdom call
to us. Wisdom offers an understanding heart.

Wisdom speaks of excellent things — excelling the
average way of handling life. Jesus is *"...the wisdom
of God."* (1 Cor 1:24) God has given His people the
mind of Christ. We are to yield to the
understanding He gives us, ignoring our own
understanding. When He opens His mouth He
speaks *right* things. Right things are available to be
heard and used.

Even if we lack understanding we can *become* wise.
If we listen and hear, we will understand wisdom
and have an understanding heart. The Lord loves to
give wisdom and in turn we give Him the credit for
our well-built lives.

෨ Plain ෰

For my mouth shall speak truth; and wickedness is an abomination to my lips. All the words of my mouth are in righteousness; there is nothing twisted or perverse in them. They are all plain to him that understands, and right to them that find knowledge.

Proverbs 8:7-9

It's a wonderful truth that *all* God says in His Word is in righteousness and in it there is nothing twisted or deceptive. All other sources are open game for the opinions of man, demonic inspiration or misguided conclusions. The bible is truly the voice of God in written format. We have access to trusted counsel, advice and perspective. All other sources, even Christian books and commentaries, are tainted with human opinion and assessment. His Word is pure and promises to enlighten our eyes. Because it is pure, we have to take our fill and be refreshed!

ఴ Better ఴ

Receive my instruction, and not silver; and knowledge rather than choice gold. For wisdom is better than rubies; and all the things that may be desired are not to be compared to it.

Proverbs 8:10-11

We are given a choice. We should receive instruction over silver, knowledge or gold. What does this say to the believer who chooses to earn time-and-a-half on a Sunday resulting in not being able to sit under his pastor's bible teaching? What does this say to the one who chooses to ignore the gathering together with believers giving his or her employment the consistent priority? Receiving instruction is of higher value than receiving a paycheck.

Choosing employment which competes with the wisdom God has shown us for our day-to-day lives, may diminish the quality of life the Lord would have for us. A person may think a second job will solve problems but, in fact, it could be foolish and result in the devastation of their marriage, family or health.

We do not measure choices only by financial benefits. We evaluate choices by the leading of the Holy Spirit and God's priorities for our lives. When considering options based only on financial gain, foolish choices can be made. These choices might give the devil opportunities to kill, steal and destroy.

I like the word "all" in <u>The Bible</u>. It is so all entailing. It covers everything. I don't even have to think of a specific situation the verse refers to. *All* the things that may be desired are not to be compared with wisdom. That means marriage, a home, security, good health, reputation, children, peace etc. are not to be compared with wisdom. We need to desire wisdom more than any treasure. Wisdom promises to fill our lives with precious and pleasant things.

❧ Hate ❧

*I wisdom dwell with discernment, and find out
knowledge and discretion. The fear of the LORD is to
hate evil: pride, and arrogance, and the evil way, and
the twisted mouth, do I hate.*

Proverbs 8:12-17

Choosing to regard something as evil because God
calls it evil, testifies that we value His judgment. We
can hear something funny on a show or movie and
chuckle. Evaluate whether this response is
appropriate. Is the joke dealing with things the Lord
says are sinful? Does the story line exalt foolishness
or mock righteousness? If we find pleasure in those
things choosing to enjoy them, we are not walking
in the fear of the Lord. We are taught to hate evil,
not be entertained by it.

This proverb gives us a list of some of the things that
He hates. We should make it our aim to hate pride,
arrogance, the evil way and the twisted mouth. The
first place to hate these is within our lives.
Whenever we are operating in pride or speak in any
sort of deceptive manner we must confess this as
sin. We should hate it enough to cry out to the Lord
for deliverance, determining to reject these
responses as acceptable. Another good place to start
is asking the Lord to *give* us a hatred for these
things. If we want to be like Him, we should love the
things He loves and hate the things He hates.

ᴥ Early ᴣ

Counsel is mine, and sound wisdom: I am understanding; I have strength. By me kings reign, and princes decree justice. By me princes rule, and nobles, even all the judges of the earth. I love them that love me; and those that seek me early shall find me.

Proverbs 8:14-17

The Lord has counsel. Counsel is His. This means it is His to give. Let us go to Him *first* for advice. Our prayer lives should not be out of duty, but dependence. We are privileged to have access to the One who gives reliable advice. He can show us how to love, manage money and time, parent, and walk our paths. Prayer is coming to the One who is called understanding, has strength and gives counsel.

We need to seek the Lord early. This could mean early in the day or early in a situation. We need to pray for our life partners *before* we meet them. We need to seek Him about our children's future before it happens. We need to seek Him about growing older before we do. We need to seek Him about handling matters before they show up.

He is the God who is the *"...Alpha and Omega, the beginning and the ending, says the Lord, which is, and which was, and which is to come, the Almighty."* (Rev 1:8) He is outside of time and we can approach Him about the future, trusting Him to order our steps in order to bring us to His desired end. Let us come before Him now rather than be anxious about tomorrow. Pray about tomorrow trusting Him to equip you today.

❧ Riches ❧

Riches and honor are with me; yes, durable riches and righteousness. My fruit is better than gold, yes, than fine gold; and my revenue than choice silver. I lead in the way of righteousness, in the midst of the paths of judgment: That I may cause those that love me to inherit substance; and I will fill their treasures.

Proverbs 8:18-21

Lasting riches and honor are found in Christ. He gives us better things than anything this world has to offer. We will profit when we mix our faith with His Word. The dividends can be cashed throughout our lives, never diminishing in worth or value. The Lord leads us in ways that are right and safe. He wants our lives to bring Him glory and show this world that He judges righteously. Children should see parents whose decisions are not based on temporal profit alone but on durable riches.

The Lord leads us in ways that are right and judged accurately. We must listen to His counsel and trust that along His paths are treasures and substance. Substance can be seen and built upon. The things of this world lack substance. They will always evade us and our eyes will never be satisfied. When we choose the way of the Lord and His will for our lives we may think we are lacking some things at first. In the long run we will be satisfied. The Lord will cause those of us who love Him to inherit substance. It will come to us. The Lord will fill our treasures.

❧ Order ☙

The LORD possessed me in the beginning of his way, before his works of old. I was set up from everlasting, from the beginning, or ever the earth was. When there were no depths, I was brought forth; when there were no fountains abounding with water. Before the mountains were settled, before the hills was I brought forth: While as yet he had not made the earth, nor the fields, nor the highest part of the dust of the world. When he prepared the heavens, I was there: when he set a compass upon the face of the depth: When he established the clouds above: when he strengthened the fountains of the deep: When he gave to the sea his decree, that the waters should not pass his commandment: when he appointed the foundations of the earth: Then I was by him, as one brought up with him: and I was daily his delight, rejoicing always before him; Rejoicing in the habitable part of his earth; and my delights were with the sons of men. Now therefore hearken to me, O you children: for blessed are they that keep my ways. Hear instruction, and be wise, and refuse it not.

Proverbs 8:22-33

His wisdom is forever settled and He knows how to counsel us in life's matters. His wisdom creates things within us and is intended to bring Him glory.

God's wisdom understands the highs and lows of our lives. Whether we are *in the heavens* or *in the depths*, the wisdom of the Lord wants to speak to us about our lives and choices.

The wisdom of the Lord will often give us boundaries, just like when the Lord gave His command that the ocean waters can only go so far. He establishes boundaries for each season of our lives. He will tell us how to enjoy blessings in moderation. He will let us know what relationships and activities are out of bounds.

Our very world declares the wisdom of God. The seasons, continents, climate, position of the sun from the earth, habitations designed for specific creatures and the rotation of the earth around the sun, all speak of perfect wisdom. These declare a God who knows how to cause all things to work together for good.

If wisdom was so foundational for all of creation, how much more do we need to ask for wisdom in the design of our lives and days? Let us ask the Lord throughout this day for His boundaries and His priorities. Let's not trust our first inclinations, but know His ways are higher than our ways. Let us be quiet and receptive to His leading, trusting that His wisdom creates beautiful things.

✌ Daily ✍

Blessed is the man that hears me, watching daily at my gates, waiting at the posts of my doors.

Proverbs 8:34

Wisdom can be heard and wisdom will be given. Wisdom is given to all who watch *daily* at the Lord's gates and wait at the posts of His doors. Are we continuing to make decisions based upon our own reasoning without coming before God asking for counsel and wisdom? Are we barreling into our days with lists of things to do, determining priorities without coming before Him in the morning watching, waiting and listening?

The Lord has so much wonderful wisdom to give us as mothers, fathers, sons, daughters, businessmen, budgeters, domestic engineers, students and employees. We are promised that we will be blessed if we hear and wait for wisdom rather than jump into things impulsively.

Let us be in a constant place of knowing that wisdom doesn't come from *within*, but descends from *above*. Let us be people who know where our help comes from. We should not jump into things before we hear wisdom speak.

❧ Find ☙

For whoever finds me finds life, and shall obtain favor of the LORD. But he that sins against me wrongs his own soul: all they that hate me love death.

Proverbs 8:35-36

When we determine God's way of doing things we find life. We shouldn't be stubborn, seeking to run our own lives. This grieves His heart and we trouble our souls. Our emotions, wills, and intellect, will experience unnecessary torment by going against the counsel of the Lord.

Foolish people, who don't want to hearken to His counsel, are loving death. Choices that contradict His counsel, drain life from those who make them. This will bring about a numb and calloused life.

We need to watch, wait, hear and find what the Lord has to say to us about every area of our lives. We must not make reckless choices that disregard God's counsel. Humbling ourselves and asking for the fear of Lord will facilitate lives well lived. If we hate the wisdom God has for us, we hurt ourselves. Making foolish and sinful choices brings death and devastation. He wants us to find life and live in His favor.

೮ Proven ೮

*Wisdom has built her house, she has carved out her
seven pillars: She has killed her beasts; she has
mingled her wine; she has also furnished her table.
She has sent forth her maidens: she cries upon the
highest places of the city, Whoever does not think
before he acts, let him turn in here: as for him that
lacks understanding, she says to him, Come, eat of
my bread, and drink of the wine which I have mingled.
Forsake foolishness, and live; and go in the way of
understanding.*

Proverbs 9:1-6

The wisdom and instruction that the Lord wants to
give us has a proven record. His instructions for our
lives build our homes and lives with strong support
and sure position. His wisdom kills those things that
want to come into our lives and devour all that He
has done for us. His wisdom is incomparable to any
sort of trendy advice offered by the "experts" of our
time.

Even when we might entertain foolish pursuits, His
voice is speaking. He is crying at the high places of
the city, beckoning us to forsake foolish living and
go in the way of our Maker.

If we find ourselves at a loss for direction, we should
turn toward the Lord and eat of *His* bread. Let's
open the Word of God with hunger being counseled
and directed. Just because we lack understanding,
we are not disqualified from experiencing a blessed
life. Rather, we should take our empty cups to the
fountain of life and be filled. Sometimes when we
lack wisdom we listen better to the Lord and we are
not so tempted to lean on our own understanding.

Foolish living depletes us of life. When we stay up too late, are lazy in our work, talk too much, spend money we don't have, commit to things the Lord never asked us to do and squander our resources, we end up drained and weary. We must forsake these natural choices, choosing to go toward an upward call of God in Christ Jesus. The Lord has saved us to show the world what a life surrendered to Christ and His wisdom can be like. Let us travel on the paths of understanding enjoying roads that are much smoother than those paved with foolishness.

൫ Scorners ൭

He that corrects a scorner gets to himself shame: and he that corrects a wicked man only harm himself. Do not correct a scorner, or he will hate you: rebuke a wise man, and he will love you. Give instruction to a wise man, and he will be yet wiser: teach a just man, and he will increase in learning.

Proverbs 9:7-8

A "scorner" is one who mocks wisdom and is wise in his or her own eyes. When someone is operating out of pride we must be careful how we give instruction and correction. When children are arrogantly stating their position as young teens, parents must be careful about giving instruction. At that moment, teens are arrogant and their hearts are hardened. Parents must still give them the Lord's standard, but correction involves not only the standard, but instruction in righteousness. When parents discern scornful dispositions in their children, limited teaching should take place. Parents should lift the standard, state the consequences and wait until their hearts soften to instruct them in the way they should go.

If we try to instruct people when their hearts are hardened we will only harm ourselves. Most likely we will succumb to the temptation of anger and wrath because our words are not finding a place in their hearts. We can discern a scornful frame of mind by observing body language, verbal responses and tone of voice.

Pray for their hearts to be softened. Pray they will be wise, just and increase in learning. Seeds should not be forced on hard ground. Lightly scatter the seed of the Word upon them. Anticipate His Spirit to rain upon them, softening their hearts. He is the

One who causes the Word to penetrate to the depths of their beings.

Are you a wise person? Do you receive instruction? Are you teachable? If so, you will be yet wiser and you will increase in learning. Approach the Word of God, pastoral studies and insights from Christians with an eagerness to be taught, and You will learn.

❧ One ☙

The fear of the LORD is the beginning of wisdom: and the knowledge of the holy is understanding. For by me your days will be multiplied, and the years of your life shall be increased. If you be wise, you will be wise for yourself: but if you scorn, you alone will bear it.

Proverbs 9:10-12

If we really want to know how to live we must be concerned with one voice alone. That is the voice of the Lord. We must fear the Lord. We must not fear man and what he thinks. We must not fear failure. We must not fear change and all that comes with it.

When we begin to seek out what God deems as holy, we will understand what life is all about. Knowing who the Lord is and what He thinks, brings understanding. This understanding produces a sure-footedness. We experience supernatural strength with quietness and confidence.

As followers of God, we have access to counsel that is sure and practical. Our days will be multiplied when we hear Him order our steps. He will tell us when we should go to bed, when to rise up, how to forgive, and what to expend our energy on. These are only a few of those things that can contribute to better health.

If we have the fear of man, we will live on the edge and tend to be anxious. This is hard on our frames. The peace of God will guard our hearts and minds in Christ as we pray about everything. We will chase away anxiety as we give thanks to Him in the midst of troubles. If we are mulling over things rather than coming before the Lord in prayer seeking His will, we may shorten our days due to stresses on our systems.

The wisdom we receive is for our lives and to cause us to build with the finest materials to the highest standards. If we mock what the Lord says or take it lightly, we will be the ones to bear it. So we must lift up our voices for this wisdom and know each wise choice we make will directly impact the quality of life we experience.

ೞ Loud ೮

A foolish woman is clamorous: she is simple, and knows nothing.

Proverbs 9:13

"Clamorous" means to murmur, make noise, to be troubled or to be in a commotion. When a woman lacks wisdom and interprets life based on her limited understanding, she will most likely make a lot of noise. *"Who is a wise man and endued with knowledge among you? let him show out of a good conduct his works with **meekness** of wisdom."* (James 3:13)

Wisdom from the Lord is associated with meekness — the quality of not having to draw attention to self. When someone is wise, they yield to that which is good. If a woman finds herself talking a lot about a situation she may not yet have God's wisdom on the matter. In order to not be clamorous, a woman should quiet her heart before the Lord, seeking Him to guide and counsel with His wisdom. She must not loud in her opinion, will and decisions. Being lowly in heart, humble in mind and yielded in will, guides a woman in wisdom that is sure to build her life and glorify the God who gives it.

ಶಿ Sin ೞ

For she sits at the door of her house, on a seat in the high places of the city, to call passengers who go on their ways:

Whoever lacks knowledge, let him turn in here: and as for him that lacks understanding, she says to him, stolen waters are sweet, and bread eaten in secret is pleasant. But he knows not that the dead are there; and that her guests are in the depths of hell.

Proverbs 9:14-18

Sin often calls to us throughout our days. Sin calls to us and lies to us. Sin tells us certain things are sweet and pleasant even though the Lord declares them evil and wicked. Sin often calls to us in the normal courses of our lives and presents things in half-truths.

If sin wasn't initially pleasing, we wouldn't be tempted. Yet afterwards, sin brings exponential devastation that exceeds any pleasure we may have experienced initially. We must not listen, enter or believe sin's beckoning. We must not be uninformed, but warned by wisdom, avoiding destruction that come from sinful behavior.

ஐ Sons ೞ

The proverbs of Solomon: A wise son makes a glad father: but a foolish son weighs heavily on the heart of his mother.

Proverbs 10:1

Given the fact that the Lord gave Solomon a *"... a wise and an understanding heart;..."*(I King 3:12), we can conclude King David would have been a glad father if he had been alive to see Solomon receive this request. But David, Solomon's father, died before this request was granted. Perhaps Solomon asked for this after hearing what his father's foolish choices brought about.

We don't know if David had regrets about certain choices and heaviness from foolishness in his youth. Absalom was a foolish half-brother of Solomon and Solomon may have heard of the heartbreak Absalom had caused his father.

The psalmist prayed, *"Remember not the sins of my youth, nor my transgressions: according to your mercy remember me for your goodness' sake, O LORD."* (Ps 25:7) Even if we, in our youthfulness, brought some heartache to our parents, the Lord is in the business of giving wisdom. We can now walk according to this wisdom and bring joy to our parents.

If wisdom makes a glad father and foolishness makes a mother heavy in heart, then parents must take the commission to train their children away from foolishness and into wisdom very seriously. Do they know about bed times, use of their words, financial wisdom, work ethic, entertainment choices, how to submit to authority, how to deliver messages faithfully, etc..? Have parents gone through the Proverbs to gain wisdom in order to have it to give their children? If parents leave children to their own, their hearts will be heavy.

ஐ Satisfied ௐ

Treasures of wickedness profit nothing: but
righteousness delivers from death. The LORD will not
allow the soul of the righteous to starve: but he
depletes the substance of the wicked.

Proverbs 10:2-3

We will not come out ahead if we get possessions through wicked actions. If we prioritize our lives according to the Lord's standards, our possessions will be protected. As we seek first to honor Him our souls will be satisfied. We will possess lasting riches. Our lives will be protected from decay and depletion.

When we put the Lord first and seek to do things HIS way, He will give us what we truly hunger for. He looks out for what we need — the nutrients that sustain and cause us to flourish. The Lord will satisfy our hunger with things that truly satisfy. Any hunger you and I experience must be directed toward seeking the Lord's will on the matter. As we do this we will truly be fed. We will lie down in green pastures with plenty to take in and share.

❧ Prosperity ☙

He becomes poor that deals with a lazy hand: but the hand of the diligent makes rich.

Proverbs 10:4

This principle should empower us in the financial areas of our lives. Diligence results in prosperity. We can end up lacking if we work in a half-hearted or lazy way. When we experience a shortage of provision, we can ask the Lord to search us and see *if* we have been lazy in our responsibilities.

There were seasons in our home when we were running low on finances. I stepped up my diligence in housework, laundry, preparing meals, making the beds, doing the dishes, mopping the floor, weeding the garden, schooling the children and showing up to commitments timely and prepared. I found that my employer, the Lord Jesus Christ, rewards diligence. Not only did I find myself so busy that I didn't have time to contemplate what I didn't have, but I found myself satisfied by consistent, diligent labor.

In Eccl 5:12 the Lord tells us *"The sleep of a laboring man is sweet, whether he eat little or much..."* The Lord is watching our diligence. He will provide as we are faithful in what He has asked us to do, regardless of whether we are being paid for doing it or not. We may face financial lack for many reasons, but let's be sure that it is not because of our laziness.

ೞ Harvestೞ

He who gathers crops in summer is a wise son, but he who sleeps during harvest is a disgraceful son.

Proverbs 10:5

We experience a myriad of seasons throughout our lives. We are to harvest, when it is the season to harvest. Whenever I found myself pregnant with another child I knew it was my time to harvest as much spiritual input as possible before that baby was born. I knew that soon there would be a famine for spiritual input with the feedings, ear infections, sleepless nights and devotion to that child. I went to every bible study, retreat and conference I could; storing up truths that would hold me through the season of spiritual famine I was about to face.

We never know when a spiritual drought will come upon us and we won't be able to gather the Word of God as we might have opportunity now. It is wise to soak up His teachings, promises and instruction while the harvest is accessible and we have the time to do so.

ॐ Influence ॐ

Blessings are upon the head of the just: but violence covers the mouth of the wicked. The memory of the just is blessed: but the name of the wicked shall rot.

Proverbs 10:6-7

When we live apart from the defining plan of God's Word we experience tumultuous lives without rhyme or reason. Our lives shake violently under the consequences and influences of sinful seeds we've sown. In order to have blessed lives, we need to seek Him and honor God with our choices.

Our mouths must be controlled by the Holy Spirit. Our hearts are to be filled with psalms, hymns, and spiritual songs, making melody to the Lord. We don't want wicked hearts. Wicked hearts produce behavior that can bring about violence.

The Lord wants our lives to be a blessing to others. We should want the thought of us to bring refreshment and encouragement in the lives of those around us. If we are forever meddling, gossiping or spreading lies or rumors, our names could very well turn the stomach of those who hear them mentioned.

We must be just. In order to be just we must be lovers of truth, pleasers of God and not only loyal to men. We don't want our names to rot. We should want others to be blessed when they consider our lives and words. It is in seeking to handle matters as our God says, we earn a reputation that is regarded as blessed.

ℬ Upright ℭ

The wise in heart will receive commandments: but a chattering fool shall fall. He that walks uprightly walks surely: but people will find out whose ways are twisted.

Proverbs 10:8-9

We must be open to receive God's commandments — to have them come in and become part of the fabric of our identities. If we contend with the Lord He will allow us to fall. This is intended to prove God was right and we were wrong. Our own understanding is not the best support to be leaning upon.

When we don't have anything hidden we can walk in a sure manner. If we have hidden sin, hidden agendas or unconfessed attitudes, our steps will give us away. Let us walk in the light as He is in the light and have good fellowship with one another. As you and I make upright choices, our paths will be straight and our steps sure.

❧ Joking ☙

He that winks with the eye causes sorrow: but a chattering fool shall fall.

Proverbs 10:10

A person may wink when they are joking or a making play on words. The wink of an eye can represent deception. Oftentimes when a person winks it means that whatever they just said is not absolutely true. Perhaps it was meant in jest or to tease the other person. This kind of trickery or jesting can cause sorrow. We should all be warned that teasing another to get a laugh is not the way of a follower of Christ.

The enemy would want us to waste our passion and words on insignificant matters especially those surrounding our own kingdoms and righteousness. The Lord doesn't want us to be chattering fools. May we be people whose words are carefully spoken with the purposed intent of building up one another and/or blessing the Lord. We don't want to fall. We want to stay in an upright position. Let us choose our words carefully.

☙ Digging ☚

The mouth of a righteous man is a well of life: but violence covers the mouth of the wicked.

Proverbs 10:11

A well is something which gets its water source from deep below the surface. To have mouths that are like wells, we must go below the surface of Christian standards to the very heart of Christ Himself. Do you take time to ponder His character? Do you seek Him for His purposes for your life in the things that come your way? Do you ask Him to open your eyes to His heart on a matter? The Lord Jesus says in Luke 6:45, *"A good man out of the good treasure of his heart brings forth that which is good; and an evil man out of the evil treasure of his heart brings forth that which is evil: for of the abundance of the heart his mouth speaks."* What are you filling up with before you arrive home at the end of the day? What are you putting into your heart in the morning before your family members wake up? What are you meditating on throughout your day? You will see a direct link between what you put in and what comes out.

People go to a well for refreshment and to quench their thirst. Can people come to you and receive from your mouth things that their souls is longing for? Can your friends and children come to you with frustrations, bad attitudes or wrong conclusions and receive words that can wash away the impurities? In the midst of a conversation polluted with cynicism and judgment do your words well up with gentle rebuke washing away the seeds of division in the body of Christ? Oh Lord help our mouths to be like wells today.

ଊ Hatred ଓ

Hatred stirs up conflict and drama: but love covers all sins.

Proverbs 10:12

If we find ourselves initiating conflict we might have hatred residing in our hearts. We might hate the person we are in conflict with, someone else or ourselves.

If we ignore His conviction and stay enslaved to the things He is asking us forsake, conflict and anger may arise within us. We may begin dealing with others in anger and strife. The inner conflict may manifest in outward conflict. We may take these frustrations out on others. We can ask the Spirit of God to search and show us any self-hatred or hatred toward others. This way we will be peacemakers.

Love covers all sins. It doesn't mean we don't see sin nor confront sin. Rather, that we don't want to expose sin or exaggerate its effects in someone's life. We don't bring it up over and over. We don't talk to others about it. We don't use it against others. We seek to have mercy and understanding in regards to the sin.

Let's be cleansed of hatred and show others the mercy we have been shown.

ℬ Knowledge ℭ

In the lips of him that has understanding wisdom is found: but a rod is for the back of him that doesn't have understanding. Wise men store up knowledge: but the mouth of the foolish is near destruction.

Proverbs 10:13-14

What we say tells a lot about who we *are*. Wise people don't have to tell everyone what they think or what they know. They store up insight, observations and counsel. Wise people not only know *what* to say but *when* to say it. In order to speak wisdom we must have wisdom. This wisdom comes from God and through the counsel of His Word. When we read His Word we should ask Him to reveal His heart, His judgments and His ways. We will then speak with great understanding.

When a foolish person speaks, they are actually sowing seeds of destruction. When we act foolishly we are tearing down our homes with our own words, destroying the very homes we are called to build. Oh Lord, help us be careful with our tongues and put a guard over our mouths.

໖ Strength ໕

The rich man's wealth is his strong city: the destruction of the poor is their poverty. The labor of the righteous tends to life: the fruit of the wicked to sin.

Proverbs 10:15-16

The first verse is speaking about wealth and earnings gained by hard work and prudent spending and saving. The second verse equates hard work with quality of life. If we work hard we will be satisfied with our lives no matter how much we make. Our strength will be in the fact that we worked for the Lord and He will take care of our needs. If we find ourselves lacking due to laziness, credit abuse, lack of employment from poor job performance, living beyond our means etc., we will be destroying our lives. Let us ask the Lord to search us out and show us how to be faithful, generous and diligent. May He cleanse us from the pursuit of ease. May we love working for Him.

ଋ Instruction ଋ

He is in the way of life that keeps instruction: but he that refuses correction errs.

Proverbs 10:17

We must hold on to every word of God and the wisdom He has so generously given us. We must not forget the things we have learned. The key to a blessed life is to continue in the things we have learned. This takes review and meditation. This is the way of *life*.

If we refuse correction, we will err. Ask the Lord for a sensitive spirit to His convictions and be quick to repent. We should ask Him to search us. We should receive the wounds of correction from the One who wants us to get it right. We must not harden our hearts but yield to His holy ways. Correction should be embraced. Cooperating with correction is the best way to experience this short time we have on earth.

❧ Slander ❧

*He that hides hatred with lying lips, and he that
utters a slander, is a fool.*

Proverbs 10:18

Our tongues can get us in trouble if they are not
under the control of the Holy Spirit. We can be
guilty of misrepresenting our hearts with our lips.
We must confess this as sin. Our words and the
meditations of our hearts are to be acceptable to
Him.

If we speak nicely to someone but inwardly we
despise them, we are acting as fools. We must ask
for the Lord's heart for that person. It is imperative
that we are honest before the Lord if we hate
someone. When we meet that person or talk about
the person we must be careful about what we say so
as not to hide our hatred with lying lips.

Does this mean we speak of our hatred to them or to
whomever we are speaking? Definitely not! But we
don't speak of our great affections if they are not
there. Rather, we speak God's truth about them and
if we find ourselves at a loss for words ... don't speak
at all.

๛ Words ๛

In the multitude of words there lacks not sin: but he that refrains his lips is wise.

Proverbs 10:19

The longer a conversation goes on, the higher probability someone might sin. The more words spoken, the more likely sin will occur. How long are you on the phone and why? How long are you on instant messenger and why? How many statuses really need to be posted and why? Is it time to leave that conversation because the words are not purposed with love and fellowship? Limit the length of any conversation unless you sense the Spirit leading you to continue. You will definitely cut down on the chances of gossip, slander, judgment, being misunderstood and a countless number of other sins and conflict. Pour out your heart before Him. Budget your time in human communication with a great sense of purposed speech. Approach conversation with a ready mind and knowledge that if there are too many words, especially those spoken in carelessness, sin might very well be produced.

❧ Worth ❧

The tongue of the just is as choice silver: the heart of the wicked is little worth.

Proverbs 10:20

Our words have value. The value comes from the source of our words — *the heart*. If we have just and righteous hearts our words will be like silver.

A just heart wants to do what is right. A just heart is not out to prove itself right but to discover and *do* that which is right. A righteous heart is a heart that is in right standing with God. A righteous heart is covered by the blood of Christ. A righteous heart is concerned with pleasing the Lord.

When our hearts are in this position our lips will speak words that reflect the beauty of our Lord just as choice silver reflects the image of the one looking into it. When our hearts are in this position we will speak words which people who hunger for encouragement, hope and forgiveness, will feed on. If our words are aren't shining, we can cry, *"Lord give me a just and righteous heart."*

ℬ Feed ℭ

The lips of the righteous feed many: but fools die for lack of wisdom.

Proverbs 10:21

Words are meant to feed others. If we speak the right words, many people will be fed. Our lips should speak that which God declares righteous. When friends ask for advice, we need to give them God's counsel. This will feed them and help them grow strong and spiritually healthy. We are to be people who give others what they need, not what they want. If we give people foolish counsel, we contribute to their spiritual death. Jesus said, *"Feed my sheep."* (John 21:17) May our lips speak His Words, His standards and His ways. We will then give food guaranteed to nourish and satisfy.

❧ Blessings ☙

The blessing of the LORD, makes rich, and he adds no sorrow with it.

Proverbs 10:22

When the Lord gives us a blessing it is nothing but a blessing. Every angle oozes with His fingerprints and His goodness. Not so when we go after blessings and take them ourselves without His leading and by our own might.

When we purchase something in our own willful rebellion when the Lord has said *"Not right now"*, we can be sure that there will be sorrow with it. If we are single and attempt to make a relationship happen because we think it is a blessing. we will have unnecessary sorrow associated with it.

If we stubbornly pursue blessings on our own terms, sorrow will accompany them. Don't we want blessings with no added sorrow? Let's wait on the Lord until they come from Him with *no* sorrows. He will get the glory. He does things absolutely perfectly. He uses blessings to show His love and favor in our lives.

If we have stubbornly gone after things, we must bow our hearts before Him and ask for His forgiveness and tender mercies. Let's ask Him to use the sorrows we are experiencing to build into us a great fear and reverence for His leading. Let us request His intervention to redeem and turn things around. He is compassionate and longs to get involved and be glorified in messes we have made.

৪০ Everlasting ৫

It is as a game to a fool to do mischief: but a man of understanding has wisdom. The fear of the wicked, it shall come upon him: but the desire of the righteous shall be granted. As the whirlwind passes, so is the wicked no more: but the righteous is an everlasting foundation.

Proverbs 10:23-25

We are called to be wise people. We should never consider something fun when God considers it unwise, sinful or wicked. We must seek to have our lives built with wisdom. This means even little decisions must never be made impulsively without regard to righteousness. They should never be rooted in momentary urges that compete with God's standard of what is right. If we are hasty in our decisions we might face winds and forces that can shake us to the core. Things we have built according to foolishness will not withstand the storms of life.

We are to humble ourselves, seeking God for the righteous responses in situations. This will result in the desires of our hearts being truly satisfied. This will lead to lives that may have winds, floods and waves, but will stand firm, not displaced. We will be steadfast and stable.

God's standards are forever established in heaven. The boundaries and wisdom He has for us create an everlasting foundation for our lives because they are everlasting truths. They are not the latest crazes, theories or social whims. When we build our lives on the everlasting One's counsel, we have an everlasting foundation.

ত Vinegar গ

As vinegar to the teeth, and as smoke to the eyes, so is the sluggard to them that send him.

Proverbs 10:26

When we have agreed to do a task or it is our responsibility, we need to not be lazy. If we are lazy, we will be like vinegar to the teeth and smoke in the eyes. Vinegar hurts the teeth and smoke makes the eyes burn and water. Do we want to have that kind of impact on the person for whom we are doing a task? We want to be blessings to those whom the Lord has put in our lives.

The next time we are given a task let's do it with all our might. It might help us to place a bottle of vinegar in plain sight to remind us to not be lazy in what we have been asked to do. Let's be diligent people who refuse to be sluggards.

✌ Longevity ☙

The fear of the LORD prolongs days: but the years of the wicked shall be shortened.

Proverbs 10:27

When we are more concerned about what God's desires are for us than anyone else's, we are walking in the fear of the Lord. When we are mastered by a concern to please the Lord, we will have prolonged days. The stress brought on by the expectations of others, can affect our health.

Fearing the Lord keeps us away from unwise and sinful choices that have the potential for ending our lives early. We won't be in sexually promiscuous relationships that carry the threat of disease. Alcohol won't be abused, avoiding liver concerns. Our diets will have balance and self-control helping our systems work in a healthy way.

The fear of the Lord will prolong our days. Let us walk in the fear of Him ALL our days.

❧ Results ❧

The hope of the righteous shall be gladness: but the expectation of the wicked shall perish.

Proverbs 10:28

The hope of the righteous is a hope that is founded in the Lord. We look to Him to move, comfort and provide. Our eyes are fixed on Jesus and our expectations comes from Him. When we hope in the Lord we are glad because we know He has the best plan for the situation. We are not looking to others to perform or meet our expectations. We are hoping in the Lord and His ability to deliver in ways that have never entered our minds. If we find ourselves in despair or depression, we might have our hope in someone or something else. This results in disappointment and must be remedied by transferring our hope back to the Rock and under the shadow of His wings.

Wickedness will not bring good things in our lives. The wicked end up frustrated and empty. It is in following a *good* God that we end up with *good* things. When we allow our wicked nature to direct our priorities and pursuits we end up greatly disappointed with our quality of life. If we build with His materials and by His design we will see the fulfillment of His hopes for us.

৵ Muscles ৎ

The way of the LORD is strength to the upright: but destruction shall be to the workers of iniquity.

Proverbs 10:29

Sometimes we think the way of the Lord is hard, resulting in depletion of our strength. When we choose to do things the way the Lord has said, it will result in *increased* strength. Whenever a body builder wants to build muscle strength, he or she needs resistance to build muscle tissue cells.

As we go against natural choices and choose God's way, we will initially face resistance. We must not panic! Resistance builds strength in our spirits. Let's keep going and we will find it much easier when faced with resistance the next time. Let's embrace the resistance as the Lord's means for building up our strength.

಄ Stable ಄

The righteous shall never be removed: but the wicked shall not inhabit the earth.

Proverbs 10:30

The righteous standards the Lord gives you for your life and home, build stability that you may not recognize at first. Don't worry. Keep building with every bit of counsel and wisdom you receive from the Lord. Your marriage, family and life will endure beyond fleeting passions and impulses. These try to court you away from enduring love and constant character. Every time you look to the blueprints of God's Word and build according to code, your life is being constructed to withstand the evil day that most likely will visit. Don't grow weary in well doing. Don't be impatient to throw your life together with substandard materials. Have the patience of the Master Builder. Look to Him each day to accomplish His will in you and through you. You will not be moved.

ℬ Acceptable ℭ

The mouth of the just brings forth wisdom: but the twisted tongue shall be cut out. The lips of the righteous know what is acceptable: but the mouth of the wicked speaks twistedness.

Proverbs 10:31-32

Time and time again we are exhorted by the wisdom of God about our speech. We have to talk every day. Every day there is the opportunity for our tongues to bring forth wisdom and life or destruction and foolishness. We must not have a twisted tongue. A twisted tongue is a deceitful tongue. Saying things we think *others* want to hear, *we* want others to hear or in a way that doesn't clearly represent truth, are all examples of a twisted tongue. Let us yield our tongues as instruments of righteousness today so we will bring forth wisdom and that which is acceptable. Let us yield our tongues to the control of the Holy Spirit that we might be a source of His truth to those around us.

ಖಾ Scales ೧೪

*A dishonest measurement is abomination to the
LORD: but an accurate weight is His delight.*

Proverbs 11:1

Sometimes in the marketplaces of old, a scale might
be upon the seller's table. Perhaps the amount of
grain to be purchased was placed there and an
appropriate price would be given per pound.
Dishonest sellers would unjustly weigh down the
scale so as to charge customers more than what the
buyers actually purchased. Here we see that a
dishonest measurement is an abomination to the
Lord.

We could very well be doing this in our own lives.
How do we weigh those matters that affect us? Does
a little word spoken to you become a larger burden
than it actually is? Do you measure the events of
your life by a scale falsely balanced by this world's
ideas of what is valuable? The Lord is delighted
when we weigh things justly. We must come before
Him in prayer and His Word to measure those
things that affect us.

We must not let the enemy, that deceiver, put false
weights where things are not that heavy. We must
not consider something insignificant if the Lord
deems it weighty. We mustn't let our own biases and
perspectives give us the wrong measurement in
assessing situations, relationships or events.

The next time you are facing something and
determining its impact, remember this verse. Ask
the Lord to help you weigh it justly and to remove
any false balances.

When you go to a gas station you will see a sticker
on the pump assuring its integrity by a

governmental agency that checks scales and measuring devices. You only want to pay for what you put in and you appreciate the integrity of an honest scale. We don't need to be weighed down by things that are judged by a dishonest scale. Let us be sure to always come before His inspection to maintain an honest way of weighing matters.

ဢ Shame ß

When pride comes, then comes shame: but with the
lowly is wisdom.

Proverbs 11:2

When we are operating with *self* on the throne, we
are bound to say or do something foolish —
something that will cause us shame. Lowliness is
best exemplified by our Lord Jesus Christ. He laid
aside His deserved position to become a man and
pay a debt He didn't owe. He cleared the way for us
to know Him. The quietness of a soul yielded only to
His approval hears *His* voice and hears *His* wisdom.
In the arrogance of our own understanding we are
bound to come to shame, but in the lowly place of
seeking guidance we have steps that are sure and
ordered. When we humble ourselves we are
admitting we don't know exactly what to do or how
to respond. This will prevent us from acting hastily
and making choices that will bring shame.

ℰ Steps ℂ

The integrity of the upright shall guide them: but the twistedness of transgressors shall destroy them.

Proverbs 11:3

Choosing paths that please the Lord, results in sure-footedness that allows us to enjoy the sights along the way. Life's choices must be guided by integrity so we can enjoy the journey without stumbling. Sensitive consciences are guided by the Holy Spirit's leading. Make choices, even in secret, that please the Lord.

Others may look like they have gained a lot of ground on their paths with twisted and dishonest actions. But the Lord says that the very things some use to try to get ahead, will destroy them in the end. Be sensitive to the Lord ordering your steps and don't compare your path with another's.

When you and I take steps guided with integrity we will be more confident with each step. When our steps are not straight, we will have to step around clutter that could very well impede our paths or create injury.

ೞ Protection ೮

Riches do not profit in the day of wrath: but
righteousness delivers from death.

Proverbs 11:4

Many people use financial criteria alone when making decisions disregarding other factors. We must never, as believers, allow such a guideline to be that which orders our steps. Whenever I go to funerals I never hear eulogies concerning the person's possessions but their character, family and faith in God. Riches do not profit in the end so why let them rule while we're living?

Do you need extra money or does your child need your time? Do you need to purchase a high maintenance item or do you need a more disciplined prayer life? Do you need to get a second job, or do you need more time investing in relationships? Ask Your Lord. He will tell you.

❧ Contrast ☙

The righteousness of the mature shall direct his way: but the wicked shall fall by his own wickedness. The righteousness of the upright shall deliver them: but transgressors shall be taken in their own wickedness. When a wicked man dies, his expectation shall perish: and the hope of unjust men perishes. The righteous is delivered out of trouble, and the wicked comes in his place.

Proverbs 11:5-8

Righteousness and wickedness — two opposing character traits. When making choices we must ask if our choices are righteous. Let's contrast the two and what happens when we make decisions based on righteous or wicked principles. After looking at these lists, consider which traits would bring the quality of life you desire.

Wickedness	**Righteousness**
shame (11:2)	wisdom (11:2)
destruction (11:3)	guidance (11:3)
falling (11:5)	deliverance (11:4,6,8)
taken (11:6)	direction (11:5)
disappointment (11:7)	
trouble (11:8)	

❧ Hypocrisy ☙

A hypocrite destroys his neighbor with his mouth: but through knowledge the just shall be delivered.

Proverbs 11:9

Our mouths can be used to destroy others. We are warned about hypocrisy. "Hypocrisy" is saying or doing something that is an inaccurate representation of a situation. When we say or do what others want us to say or do, it is hypocrisy. When we say or do what will make us look good in the sight of others, we are guilty of hypocrisy. This will destroy the people around us.

If we are on the phone speaking with warmth and kindness and then turn around and snap at our children or mates, we are hypocrites. If we are quick to pray for and help others, but rarely pray or help those in our own households, we are hypocrites. We are destroying those in our homes.

Lord, may we never just play the part but be consistent in love and concern.

❧ Affirm ❧

When it goes well with the righteous, the city rejoices:
and when the wicked perish, there is shouting. By the
blessing of the upright the city is exalted: but it is
overthrown by the mouth of the wicked.

Proverbs 11:10-11

Most of us have little *cities* we impact. Moms,
employees, managers, students or dads all have
spheres of influence we could call *cities*. We must
exalt that which is righteous and cause that which is
wicked to perish and not have a voice in our *cities*.
Our *cities* will rejoice, shout and be blessed as we
filter out those attitudes, entertainment choices and
lifestyles that the Lord deems as wicked.

Oh Lord, help us affirm things you value and
disregard the lures of temporal pleasures that
conflict with Your plans for our lives. Give us
wisdom in supporting those in our worlds when they
seek first Your kingdom and Your righteousness.
May we remember to bless those who do the right
things and promote that which is valued by You!

ಕಾ Repeating ೮ಽ

He that lacks wisdom despises his neighbor: but a man of understanding holds his peace. A talebearer reveals secrets: but he that is of a faithful spirit conceals the matter.

Proverbs 11:12-13

In order to be wise we should not analyze and critique others. We must hold our peace and faithfully bring others before the Lord. Do you consistently bring those closest to you before the Lord? Might I encourage you to do so even now? Perhaps you could stop now and pray specifically for those you are closest to.

A talebearer is a story teller. We can tell someone in detail what occurred in a situation. This can be great when we are telling of the wonderful acts the Lord has done in our or others' lives. We can tell stories about others. But before we know it, we are delivering ammunition for the enemy to use in another's life. We should want to be known for having faithful spirits. When someone tells us something, let us not be eager to repeat it but enjoy it without being quick to tell others.

৪ Counselors ৫

Where no counsel is, the people fall: but in the multitude of counsellors there is safety.

Proverbs 11:14

When we need advice and are truly seeking to please the Lord, a multitude of counselors is a safe way to go. We should ask different people from different spheres of influence. We are often very biased in our own understanding and an honest look from different viewpoints will help us walk according to advice that is safe.

The key is that they would be considered *counselors* in our lives. The Word does not tell us *"In the multitude of voices there is safety."* We must consider whom we pour out our hearts to. If God has put someone in authority or influence over our lives, they may be one of those counselors. If we consider someone a mentor, whose lives we desire to pattern ours after, they may be one of those counselors.

When someone is seeking our counsel, we should ask them what advice others have given. This can help us help them listen for the Lord's voice. Knowing others' advice may give us insight into the person or situation.

Good counsel keep us safe. Safety is valuable. Safety assures us we are not going to be injured suddenly and unaware. Consider your counselors. Consider your counsel.

ೞ Borrowing ೞ

He that is collateral for a stranger shall pay for it: and he that hates being a co-signer is sure.

Proverbs 11:15

We must be very cautious about being collateral or a co-signer. When we lend to anyone, <u>The Bible</u> says to lend without expecting repayment. This means that if we commit to lend someone money we must be *willing* to not get paid. We should not lend if we are not *willing* to take a loss. If we commit ourselves as collateral for someone we have to be willing to cover if they fail to pay. The best bet is not to co-sign in order to avoid conflict in relationships. You have the right to say 'no' and save a relationship. If you pray and sense you are to come alongside someone in this manner, be willing to take the loss and keep the friendship if they fail to pay. Use wisdom.

ଏ Grace ଓ

*A gracious woman retains honor: and strong men
retain riches.*

Proverbs 11:16

A woman who is gracious is full of grace. The
gracious woman will have her steps guided by grace.

The opposite of grace is earned favor — showing
kindness and demonstrating affection based upon
performance. Women of grace treat people based on
unconditional love and not whether they live up to
certain expectations. In Galatians we read, *"Christ is
become of no effect to you, whosoever of you are
justified by the law; you are fallen from grace."* (Gal
5:4). If a woman measures the actions of others by a
set of her own standards, she ceases from being a
gracious woman.

Mothers remind their children to honor them.
Children will see their mothers as women who
deserve honor when their mothers parent with
grace. This doesn't mean mothers don't give
consequences and train them in the way they should
go. It means that mothers are rooting for them when
they discipline, desiring their success. Grace extends
opportunities for improvement, repentance and
victory. Gracious mothers are not motivated by self-
interest. They are not quick to punish their children
because the children's actions are making the
mothers' lives uncomfortable.

Women will be held in honor by their children and
those around them if they know how to speak the
truth in love. When someone gives grace and truth,
as Jesus came to give, she will be able to help others
grow. They will not be afraid of judgments or
dismayed by her lack of concern. If you find yourself

lacking grace, remember that grace and truth came by Christ. If Christ is in you, you have the resources to have these *twins* flow out of you, establishing the honor the Lord desires you to retain.

Men who seek to be strong will experience financial integrity and consistency. A man who is strong in self-control, does not give in to impulsive purchases. He will retain his riches. He will not be a man who spends his money on things that are rooted in the pride of life, lusts of the eyes or the lusts of the flesh. As a man is strong in the Lord and seeks His leading in the financial arena of his life, he will avoid unnecessary financial loss. A strong man can save and say 'no' to that which would ask him to squander his hard-earned money.

May the Lord grant us to be strong and gracious for His glory and our reputations.

❧ Trouble ☙

The merciful man does good to his own soul: but he that is cruel troubles his own flesh.

Proverbs 11:17

"Mercy" is being able to see what someone really deserves and intentionally extending forgiveness and an opportunity to try again and again in the same arena. Mercy says, "*You have sinned and I recognize it, but I forgive you. Let's start over.*"

If we do walk in mercy with others or ourselves, our very flesh will be troubled. We can have physical troubles as a direct result of lacking mercy. This can happen two ways. When we hold on to past sins others have committed against us we can trouble our flesh. When we have confessed our sin and yet carry unnecessary guilt we trouble our flesh. Do you have a high-strung personality? Do you sense tension in your neck, shoulders or jaw? Is your stomach easily troubled or do headaches plague you? Sometimes these ailments are brought on because you lack mercy. You have replayed things over and over again until you relive the pain many times over, experiencing the wounds deeper and deeper although they were inflicted only once.

Do you not know your lack of mercy is in direct conflict with the One who now resides within you? Do you not know you are cooperating with your adversary and aiding him in your destruction? Right now, bring that offense before the cross. Let the mercy of the blood of Christ be applied to that offense. It is more powerful than the offense itself! Cry out for forgiveness for your hardened heart and allow the Spirit of God to turn your heart of stone back into the tender heart of flesh you once had.

❧ Wicked ❧

The wicked works a deceitful work: but to him that plants seeds of righteousness shall be a sure reward. As righteousness tends to life: so he that pursues evil pursues it to his own death. They that are of a twisted heart are an abomination to the LORD: but such as are upright in their way are his delight. Though hand join in hand, the wicked shall not be unpunished: but the seed of the righteous shall be delivered.

Proverbs 11:18-21

Just as wickedness produces certain results, so does righteousness. We can tend to focus on the negative consequences of sinful choices and ignore the positive consequences of righteous choices. Whatever we plant, we reap. This means that if we plant seeds in our lives that are of His ways, we shall reap a wonderful harvest. Seeds take a while to grow. When we commit certain sins we sometimes don't reap for many years — so, too, with righteousness. We may not see and feast on the wonderful harvest until time passes. Be patient. Keep planting. You will reap in due season if you do not give up.

೫ Clothing ೫

As a ring of gold in a swine's snout, so is a beautiful woman which is without discretion.

Proverbs 11:22

A ring of gold is very beautiful but not appreciated when placed upon the snout of a swine. Though its intrinsic worth and beauty remains, its inappropriate placement makes it look ridiculous and repulsive.

Women have so many wonderful opportunities to enhance their physical appearance. Women even notice other women who are strikingly beautiful. This privilege comes with responsibility. If women draw undue attention to the flesh they become those gold rings in pigs' noses.

Women can pray over their wardrobe — each article of clothing. They could ask the Lord if they are appropriate for a woman who professes that her affections are on the things above and not on the things of the earth. If there is doubt, throw it out!

ℰ Generosity ℰ

The desire of the righteous is only good: but the
expectation of the wicked is wrath. There is that
which scatters, and yet increases; and there is that
which withholds more than is appropriate, but leads
to poverty. The generous soul shall be made fat: and
he that waters shall be watered also himself. He that
withholds corn, the people shall curse him: but
blessings shall be upon the head of him that sells it.

Proverbs 11:23-26

So much of our financial wellbeing is directly tied to
the laws/principles that the Lord has established
within creation. The opposite rule often applies to
that which springs forth in our lives. If we give, we
receive. If we die then we live. If we lower ourselves,
we will be lifted up. When we become channels
through which God can bless others, He seems to
pour more through us.

Many believers do not understand this. We often
rely on the wisdom of the world and wonder why it
just doesn't work. One of the financial priorities God
established in the Old Testament was the tithe.
When we realize that the first tenth of all our labors
belongs to the Lord and we are the vessels through
which He sends this for His work, we will begin to
see His faithfulness and provisioning.

The Lord tells us in Malachi 3:10-11: *"Bring all the*
tithes into the storehouse, that there may be meat in my
house, and prove me now, says the LORD of hosts, if I
will not open you the windows of heaven, and pour out a
blessing, that there shall not be room enough to receive
it. And I will rebuke the devourer for your sakes, and he
shall not destroy the fruits of your ground; neither shall
your vine cast her fruit before the time in the field, says
the LORD of hosts."

I have heard countless testimonies as well as experienced myself the faithfulness of God when the tithe is priority. Do you prioritize earthly government by being sure to pay taxes and yet neglect the kingdom of God? Prayerfully consider your giving. Prayerfully consider the flow of your finances.

May we honor the Lord with our substance and be more concerned with financing His kingdom than our own.

ಱ Favor ೮

He that diligently seeks to do good receives favor: but he that seeks mischief, it shall come to him.

Proverbs 11:27

Sometimes we live in a non-seeking manner. We exist with little motivation to pursue *anything*. This is usually due to a lack of focus and understanding of why we were created. The Lord tells us in Ephesians 2:10, *"For we are his workmanship, created in Christ Jesus for good works, which God has before ordained that we should walk in them."* We should wake up and seek *good*. What works has God prepared for us to walk in?

If we diligently seek *good* we will receive favor. This word favor implies smoother relationships than if we had not sought *good* diligently. Even in marriages the Lord instructs a virtuous woman to *"...do him good and not evil all the days of her life."* (Prov 31:12)

Whether at work or in our home, may we do others good and trust that favor follows those who actively do *good* to others.

༮ Flourish ༃

*He that trusts in his riches shall fall: but the
righteous shall flourish as a branch.*

Proverbs 11:28

We must not look at our bank balances as the net
that would catch us should we have financial
trouble. We must look to the Lord and know even if
we have money, it is the Lord that has brought it our
way. If we always goes back to what we *own* as a
place we find our peace, the Lord warns us that we
will fall.

This doesn't necessarily mean that our riches will
fail but we will *fall*. It means riches cannot deliver us
when we face a myriad of challenging trials. When
someone is facing unfaithfulness in their marriage, a
terminal illness or a rebellious child, riches cannot
be trusted to deliver.

We must remember that God's blessings on us are
wonderful. His provision brings us things we need,
things we want, provision for His work and to bless
others. God did not intend these things to be our
security or confidence.

Choosing to do the right thing as a righteous person
will help us, remain flourishing, stable and secure in
whatever trying times we face. We must realign any
confidence we may have put in what we *own* and
place it in the God who wants to direct our
responses in a righteous and secure way.

This way we will not *fall* but, rather *flourish!*

❧ Inheriting ❧

He that troubles his own house shall inherit the wind:
and the fool shall be servant to the wise of heart.

Proverbs 11:29

Wind is not something we can really put our hands on. Wind coming upon us is rather shaking, displacing and oftentimes loud. The Lord warns that if we are the ones who trouble our houses we shall inherit the wind. This word "trouble" means, to stir up or afflict. We must guard our tongues and hearts. Much of what many are troubled by within their home is actually that which they have planted.

Be careful! God has given us an influence over the climate of the home. Let's not stir things up! Inheriting the wind means we never truly grasp a solid sense of blessing. Life seems to go by with nothing to show for it. So much of what the Lord wants us to experience is based on what we plant. Let's not be foolish and end up with unnecessary regrets and lack the substantial inheritance the Lord has for us.

❧ Eternal ☙

The fruit of the righteous is a tree of life; and he that wins souls is wise. Behold, the righteous shall be recompensed on the earth: much more the wicked and the sinner.

Proverbs 11:30-31

Much of Proverbs deals with wisdom. One of the ways we can be wise is by being concerned about the eternal destination of those around us. Do you have a tender heart toward those who have yet to know Christ as their Savior and Lord? Do you pray regularly for those who are yet dead in their trespasses and sins? Do your children know the plan of salvation and that you desire their names to be written in the Lamb's Book of Life above all other dreams you may have for them?

Besides being concerned about the eternal destination of others, God deals with us here and now. Do you also know if you choose the right thing you shall be recompensed *on* the earth? Perhaps not immediately, but every righteous choice we make is certain to bring forth fruit. Have the patience of a farmer and continue planting choices that please and honor God. You will eventually reap a wonderful, delicious harvest.

&0 Teachable C&

Whoever loves instruction loves knowledge: but he that hates correction is stupid.

Proverbs 12:1

A good teacher is one who wants to learn. A teacher who doesn't mind being corrected, is a teacher whose students will love learning. Sometimes a parent will try to teach their children and wonder why they don't seem excited to learn from them. Children should see their parents' love for instruction. What does a child's parent do when they are corrected? Does the parent enjoy researching and learning new things?

Are you more concerned with learning things accurately or just spouting off your opinion? Do you have newly acquired insights about the world, the Word of God or some truth? When others share something they learned, do you rejoice with them and ask them questions?

Maturity and transformation comes from correction. To be a person who loves instruction is to be one who loves knowledge. Learning keeps us in a place of humility and brings great discovery. We will be much easier to get along with when we don't think we know everything.

ജ Rooted ☙

A good man obtains favor from the LORD: but a man
of wicked devices will he condemn. A man shall not be
established by wickedness: but the root of the
righteous shall not be moved.

Proverbs 12:2-3

When a palm tree faces hurricane-force winds, the
tree will bend and leaves may depart. It will not be
uprooted and eventually straightens back up and re-
grows the palms that keep it a landmark for all to
see. The palm tree will have to regain composure
and be healed a bit from the effects of the storm but
remains positioned and established.

"The righteous shall flourish like a palm tree..." (Ps
92:12) As we seek to do things righteously we will
not be moved. No matter what is thrown our way, or
how we may bend to the point of almost breaking, if
we have established our responses by the Lord's
standards, we will not be moved. Endure with the
Lord's leading and you will find yourself standing
strong again, positioned and gaining back those
things that may have departed during your
hurricanes.

☙ Crowns ❧

A virtuous woman is a crown to her husband: but she that makes ashamed is as rottenness in his bones.

Proverbs 12:4

A woman can shame her husband by living in a way that is not virtuous. Exposure to examples that exalt immorality, flirtatiousness, immodesty, deceit and other evil actions, could cause a woman to admire wicked qualities. She could devalue the virtues that are to be a crown to her husband. She must be careful to take in sources that exalt noble qualities. Women can be seduced into thinking things that are noble are worthless and things that will be judged are admirable. Women need God to evaluate and direct the influences in their lives so husbands can be crowned by their virtues.

When a husband has a virtuous wife, he gains honor from others. If a man asks his wife to compromise a moral standard, he is injuring his own position as head of the family. When a woman has noble virtues and her husband affirms and appreciates them, she becomes a crown to him, causing him to carry out his role in a royal way.

ᛒ Standards ᛩ

*The thoughts of the righteous are right: but the
counsels of the wicked are deceit. The words of the
wicked are to lie in wait for blood: but the mouth of
the upright shall deliver them. The wicked are
overthrown, and are not: but the house of the
righteous shall stand. A man shall be commended
according to his wisdom: but he that is of a perverse
heart shall be despised.*

Proverbs 12:5-8

The Lord has given us the mind of Christ. Rather
than listening to the counsels of the wicked, we
should be quiet enough to hear His leading within
us confirmed by His Word. The counsels of the
wicked are found in television, magazines, websites,
non-Christian co-workers and family members as
well as books. We need to meditate on the Word of
the Lord and allow His Word to be a lamp to our
feet and a light to our paths.

Perversion produces foolishness. Righteousness
produces wisdom. If we are to be esteemed wise we
had best stay close to the commandments of God. In
Psalm 119:30 we learn we are to lay *His* judgments
before us. We must make a time to focus and expose
ourselves to *His* counsels. This will result in
priorities and choices that are wise and endure time.

If we are inconsistent and twisted in our standards,
the scriptures say we will be despised. In order to be
held in honor we need to have standards rooted in
the wisdom of God. If we twist things and are
inconsistent, we could frustrate others and they will
despise us. "Perversion" means "to twist." Let us stay
in His Word and have standards true to the
everlasting commands of God, causing us to be

people who are commended according to our
wisdom.

ℬ Character ℭ

He that is despised, and has a servant, is better than he that honors himself, and lacks bread.

Proverbs 12:9

Sometimes we want to give off a good impression regardless of the state of our beings. The Lord Jesus never concerned himself with other people's opinions. He focused on pleasing the Father and was so confident in who He was that even when they called Him "Beelzebub", the prince of devils, He was not shaken nor needed to defend Himself.

Our true worth is *not* defined by the evaluation of *others*. We may want to appear one way in the eyes of others to give us a sense of importance or worth. This causes us to be hypocrites. We are seeking to honor ourselves.

The true evaluation of our character is what we really *have* in our character *not* what we want others to *think* we have. We may present ourselves in a purposefully slanted way on social media. We might use this to convince ourselves that we are doing better than we are really are. We may honor ourselves and try to appear as something we are not only to discover when we are alone that we are lacking the very things we wanted others to think we have.

We are not to decide what to say or do based on whether people will be impressed or bothered. We are to live in a way that pleases God *even* if others despise us for it.

When we speak up for what is right we may find ourselves despised. When we do what is right we will come out ahead. Righteousness will establish us and give us enduring riches. We must focus on

doing the will of God rather than exalting ourselves
in the eyes of others.

ᘒ Animals ᗍ

A righteous man regards the life of his beast: but the tender mercies of the wicked are cruel.

Proverbs 12:10

Animals were created by the Lord and put here intentionally. In the beginning the Lord gave Adam the privilege of naming the animals. *"And out of the ground the LORD God formed every beast of the field, and every fowl of the air; and brought them to Adam to see what he would call them: and whatsoever Adam called every living creature that was its name."* (Gen 2:19).

The Lord gave Adam and Eve authority over the animals. We are accountable for what we do with this responsibility. Do we neglect the care of our household pets? Do we loathe animals that the Lord entrusted us with? Do we idolize our pets and have them rule over us? A righteous man cares for the needs of his beast and esteems this dominion as God-given and a commission he or she must handle faithfully.

ஐ Cultivate ൽ

He that tills his land shall be satisfied with bread: but
he that follows aimless people lacks understanding.
The wicked desires the net of evil men: but the root of
the righteous yields fruit.

Proverbs 12:11-12

If we till our lands we shall be satisfied. Sometimes
we find ourselves not satisfied or sensing we haven't
had enough of something. We thirst and hunger and
don't know why. One remedy for this is tilling our
lands. How have you been tending to your dishes,
laundry, dusting, making the beds, gardening,
cooking, home projects, yard work, paying bills, car
repairs etc.? Do you find yourself procrastinating on
tilling your land and then wandering from store to
store, or this snack to this snack hoping something
will settle you down? Try tilling your land.

Instead of eating food when you aren't hungry, go
do a chore. Instead of going to the mall, clean out a
cabinet. Instead of watching the game, take out the
trash. Working and laboring God-given assignments
surprisingly brings about a strong sense of
satisfaction. *"The sleep of a laboring man is sweet,*
whether he eat little or much..." (Eccl 5:12a).

Satisfaction is linked to labor. Our Father in heaven
is letting us know one remedy for discontentment,
restlessness and perhaps depression would be to
evaluate our areas of responsibility and take care of
them. When a farmer tills the land they prepare the
land to go from dirt to a harvest. What harvest does
the Lord want to bring about in your areas of
responsibility? Let us be people who are diligent
with the land God has given us and experience a
sense of satisfaction. This will come from labor-
filled days and tilling the land He has given us.

ಎಂ Satisfaction ೮೩

The wicked is snared by the transgression of his lips:
but the just shall come out of trouble. A man shall be
satisfied with good by the fruit of his mouth: and the
recompense of a man's hands shall be rendered to
him.

Proverbs 12:13-14

Our mouths oftentimes direct the flow of our days
and relationships. Satisfaction comes from the fruit
of our mouths. What kinds of things are you saying
to those in your home, co-workers or even to
yourself? Many times conflict and strain in
relationships results from the wrong words being
spoken.

Satisfaction can come from what we say. Perhaps
some sense of discontent is brooding in your life
because your mouth was used in the wrong way. If
that is true, recognize it, ask for forgiveness and seek
God as to how to make things right. Much trouble is
brought about by our mouths and much satisfaction
is intended to come from the good of our mouths.
Ask the Lord to put a guard over your mouth and to
speak through you to everyone today.

ꙮ Hearken ꙮ

The way of a fool is right in his own eyes: but he that hearkens to counsel is wise.

Proverbs 12:15

When we are confident in ourselves we are most likely playing the fool. If we are confident in the Lord's counsel through His Word and basing our confidence upon His precepts, we are wise. When in a disagreement within yourself or with another, maintain humility and be open to correction. The Lord gives grace to the humble but resists the proud.

Listening to counsel is not the same as *hearkening* to counsel. We can expose ourselves to the best bible studies, books and influences and still remain fools. May the Lord give us the ability to *hearken* to counsel — to adjust ourselves to the Lord's counsel and take it as we would a prescription.

"I thought about MY ways, and turned my feet to YOUR testimonies" (Ps 119:59).

ঔ Prudence ৎ

A fool's wrath is presently known: but a prudent man covers shame. He that speaks truth shows forth righteousness: but a false witness deceit.

Proverbs 12:16-17

Prudence is an old-fashioned word. It is being able to decide on the right thing to do at any given moment regardless of feelings, natural bents, or even the influences and pressures of people or culture.

People cannot predict what a prudent person will do based solely on their personality. He hears the leading of the Holy Spirit and obeys. Those around him notice he seems to know what to do in most situations. A prudent person covers shame. He doesn't talk about the failings and mistakes of others in a way to make himself look good or to prove himself right. He looks out to present people in the best light according to truth. He purposes to believe all things and hope all things. He walks in love.

๛ Swords ଔ

There is a person who speaks like the piercings of a sword: but the tongue of the wise is health. The lip of truth shall be established for ever: but a lying tongue is but for a moment. Deceit is in the heart of them that imagine evil: but to the counsellors of peace is joy. There shall no evil happen to the just: but the wicked shall be filled with mischief.

Proverbs 12:18-21

These are contrasting proverbs. They show the differences of two different ways of living. These are mutually exclusive attributes. They are dealing with the tongue, truth, deceit and being just. So much of how we live is decided upon mutually exclusive responses.

If we are tearing down, we are *not* building up. If we are lying or twisting the truth, we are *not* walking in truth. If we are being wicked, we are *not* being just. If we are walking in the Spirit, we are *not* fulfilling the lusts of the flesh.

Our tongues contribute to the health of our relationships. If we speak wise words, communication will be better. Whenever our words pierce or wound, we are not using the tongue of the wise. Cutting words will produce unhealthy relationships requiring constant attention and infecting all those around them. Do you want your marriage to be healthy? Do you want your communication with your children to be full of life and health? Do you want your friendships to be thriving and functioning at their best? Go with the tongue of wisdom and forsake piercing words. The tongue of the wise is health.

ஐ Abomination ௸

Lying lips are an abomination to the Lord, But He delights in those who deal truthfully.

Proverbs 12:22

When we think of abominations, lying doesn't usually make the list. We think of perverted actions, blaspheme and vile conduct as abominations. The Lord esteems lying as an abomination. He is the Truth and in Him there is no darkness. He is not a deceiver and He speaks truth. When we lie we come against the very nature and character of God. No matter how small the lie might be, it is still an abomination. We need to understand God's position on this so we take lying seriously. Our consciences need to be highly sensitive to any lie we might speak or be tempted to speak if we are living to please the Lord.

When we are honest we bless the Lord. He delights in the person who speaks the truth. To speak the truth consistently we must love the truth more than we care about consequences of speaking truth. If we love the Lord, we should love what He loves. He loves truth. He wants us to reflect His nature. When we live truthfully we are conduits of the Spirit of Truth. Truth is to be valued. Truth is to be esteemed. As we deal truthfully, we delight the Lord.

ଈ Conceal ଔ

A wise and discerning person conceals knowledge, but the heart of fools proclaims foolishness.

Proverbs 12:23

If we are wise, we will not have to display our wisdom. Wisdom is able to be quiet. When we are people who are seeking to please the Lord in deed, thought and lifestyle, we seek to store up knowledge within us.

Wisdom takes time and experience to own. When we observe, listen and judge with His mind, we realize our first assessments are not mature enough to speak. We live in a proven way without words. Our choices will speak more than our words. We can keep things between us and the Lord until we sense His leading to speak. We are more focused on doing the right things than proclaiming we are right.

Foolish living is accompanied with many words. Debates, boasting, and justifying are found in the mouths of fools. Foolish living needs an audience.

Lord, help us aspire to lead quiet, wise lives honoring You. May Your Words be seen through our choices. Help us to be quiet in our thoughts and words. Let our lives speak loudly of who You are. When we get too talkative show us if foolishness is near.

❧ Labor ☙

The hand of the diligent will rule, But the lazy man will be forced to labor.

Proverbs 12:24

Working diligently marks us as candidates for promotion. Many people start out strong at a job only to sputter out. Fervency becomes apathy. Promptness becomes tardiness. A team player becomes self-seeking. A diligent employee works consistently and fervently. They will work hard regardless of position or pay. Their performance is reliable and contributing. This type of employee will be promoted and respected.

The lazy employee will end up with the tasks and assignments no one wants to do. After doing minimal work, they are not given the tasks that require diligence. They must work harder for less money. Their laziness has caused them to lose respect, position and opportunities.

The Lord wants us to work diligently. We can move up from hard labor to overseer positions. If we are lazy we can end up losing our jobs and having to work jobs that are more grunt work than ruling. Diligence promotes. Laziness gets us nowhere.

❧ Anxiety ❧

Anxiety in the heart of man causes depression, but a good word makes it glad.

Proverbs 12:25

Anxiety can come from forecasting problems in the future. By predicting outcomes a person can be brought to a place of panic. It is good to be prepared for the worst but quite another to panic. God is the One who sees the future and is the One who is able to see it *and* handle it. We are not given grace in the present to handle our futures. When we get there, He will give us what we need. Anxiety can bring depression because people are borrowing troubles from tomorrow. This produces a dread of the future and a sense of hopelessness. God loves us and gives us what we need when we need it. It is important for us to come back to the moment and trust the great I AM to strengthen us in the immediate. As we trust in Him for this we will come to trust Him to do the same in the future.

A good word will help depressed hearts. This can be from a friend, the scriptures or other sources. By taking in good words, people guard themselves against depression rooted in anxiety. Knowing God's promises, listening to His praises and hearing of His faithfulness in others' lives all bring good words to anxious hearts.

Lord, help us be instruments to speak these good words. Show us if we are depressed due to anxiety. Lead us to good words that will make us glad.

౬ Choose ఆ

*The righteous should choose his friends carefully, for
the way of the wicked leads them astray.*

Proverbs 12:26

God gives mankind free will — the ability to choose.
Many people surround us. We have neighbors, do-
workers, classmates and family. We don't have
authority over who moves next door to us. We don't
choose our family members. We choose our friends.

We make choices in who we consider companions
and confidantes. We are greatly influenced by the
people we are surrounded by. This should awaken
us to a sense of caution and responsibility in
choosing friends. God wants us to be careful in
choosing friends. When we are comfortable with
someone we are influenced by them. They give us
advice, make suggestions for fun and their lives
merge with ours.

We can learn a lot about how a friend affects us by
considering what happens when we spend time with
them. Do we leave with regrets for things we've
heard from them, said to them or done with them?
Are we better people because they are in our lives?
Do we see things we admire in them?

Lord, give us insight to choose friends that fulfill
Your Word that two are better than one.

ᘒ Finish ᘓ

The lazy man does not roast what he took in hunting.
But diligence is man's precious possession.

Proverbs 12:27

Many people enjoy hunting. Setting out to find the animal, strategizing how to hunt it and then celebrating the kill all contribute to a great experience for the hunter. Then, they must bring home the animal and start the dirty work. The hide must be cut off and the meat separated from the inedible parts. This is not as fun as the hunt itself.

We are lazy if we refuse to do what it takes to see something through to its completion. If we purchase groceries and then go out to eat because we don't want to dirty the dishes and cook, we are like this hunter. If we buy a new car and then refuse to maintain it we are lazy. If we like to start new projects and not complete them we are lazy. If we run from situations that are messy and involve labor, we are like this hunter.

God, help us be like You. You don't just start things, You finish them. You are the Author and the Finisher. We pray our lives would pattern who You are. Amen.

ঙ Life ন্ড

In the path of righteousness is life, and in its pathway there is no death.

Proverbs 12:28

The wages of sin is death. Doing what is right brings life. We can contribute to the health of our emotions, relationships and environments. We do this by making righteous choices. God's laws are based on what contributes to life. He is the One who gave us life and knows what propagates life. By aligning our values with His righteous judgments we are promised lives that mature and get stronger. Every time we choose to do what is right we bring life to our paths. We may not see it initially but life will come. Relationships will be protected from decay. Our perspectives will be filled with hope. Activities will flourish with joy. Our jobs will have a sense of purpose. Life is good. The paths of righteousness are filled with life. We may have to die to our own desires but these deaths will bring lasting life to our paths.

Lord, help us remember Your ways are the way of life. Thank You for giving us Your Word so we can know what is righteous.

❧ Parents ☙

A wise son hears his father's instruction: but a scorner doesn't hear rebuke.

Proverbs 13:1

The Lord has put our parents in our lives to instruct us. Some of our fathers have instructed us by the good examples and excellent words of wisdom they have given us. Others have experienced the instruction of a bad example and foolish counsel. Either way we can be instructed. The key is hearing instruction from either type of father. Even if our fathers were never in our lives we can hear the instruction in that example as well.

Your life is precious to your Lord. He can take every dynamic you've experienced and use it for your good. If you will quiet your own understanding and ask the Lord to help you hear your father's instruction, you will be a wise person. Your father's instruction is intended to cause you to be all the Lord wants you to be.

❧ Digest ☙

A man shall eat good by the fruit of his mouth: but the soul of the transgressors shall eat violence. He that keeps his mouth keeps his life: but he that opens wide his lips shall have destruction.

Proverbs 13:2-3

Much of what we ingest in our days is a direct result of what and how we say things. We cannot fully comprehend the power of the tongue. We would do well to absorb whatever truths the Lord gives us concerning our tongues. There is a contrast between a mouth that is used correctly and the soul of a sinner. People who are entangled and walking in sin will have mouths of anger, blame and violence. Most fights start with words that push the right button.

If the Holy Spirit is clearly showing you a transgression, repent! If you don't, you will begin to speak violent words and spill out things that destroy, if you haven't done so already. Guilt produces anger. Guard your mouth. Guard your life. Eat *good* and keep your life. Avoid violence and destruction.

"For in many things we offend all. If any man offend not in word, the same is a mature man, and able also to bridle the whole body." (James 3:2).

&o Satisfied c&

The soul of the sluggard desires, and has nothing: but the soul of the diligent shall be made fat.

Proverbs 13:4

Part of the soul is the will — the ability to choose. Our souls can desire things and think about things to the point that discontentment settles in and a defeatist attitude follows.

If we are lazy, our souls will tend to desire things and do nothing about it. If we are not tending to our responsibilities, we will begin to focus on what we don't have. If we are hard workers we *will* recognize and appreciate what the Lord has given us and done for us.

If you are struggling with or desire to avoid a restless, lacking soul, look around. Go do those dishes. Mop that floor. Fold and put away that laundry. Wash those walls. Wash the car. Make your bed. Clean that bathroom. Do something with diligence and watch your inner man begin to feel full and satisfied.

ಶ Repulsed ಚ

A righteous man hates lying: but a wicked man is loathsome, and comes to shame.

Proverbs 13:5

If we are longing to live the way the Lord wants us to live, we will be repulsed when truth is misrepresented. We are not going to just mentally acknowledge that something is not true. We will position ourselves against deceit and lies. Lies will not be welcomed within us or around us. The smallest compromise of the truth will not sit well with us.

If we *hate* some sort of food we will not eat it. If we *accidentally* ate a hated food, we would spit it out abruptly and passionately. So, too, we should handle any lies we hear or speak.

❧ Protection ☙

*Righteousness keeps him that is upright in the way:
but wickedness overthrows the sinner.*

Proverbs 13:6

We can be tempted to be inconsistent in right choices. Maybe our church attendance or daily times in prayer or the Word of God are challenged by forces seeking to interrupt righteousness. When we are clear about the right things to do and we continue in them, these disciplines will keep us in the way. We will not be misled. We will be kept from wandering and aimless pursuits. We will be *kept* in the way — protected from slippery paths that lead to destruction and harm.

ଡ Riches ଓ

There is one who makes himself rich, yet has nothing: there is he that makes himself poor, yet has great riches.

Proverbs 13:7

Seeking to be rich is never to be the main pursuit in a believer's life. Proverbs 23:4 tells us *"Labor not to be rich ..."* Riches and honor are from the Lord. There are so many proverbs that admonish us to work hard, uprightly and not to be lazy. We focus on *how* we work and not *what* we receive from working.

Wealth is measured by God's standard and His standard alone. The riches we have in seeking first His kingdom are bountiful and never touched by a thief or corrupted by moth or rust. Sometimes we make decisions that will not financially benefit us but we find other deposits in the account of our character.

Child of God, enjoy the riches of His grace today. Praise Him for all He is to you and seek to make decisions to further His kingdom, trusting Him to bless you appropriately.

৪০ Light ৫৪

The ransom of a man's life are his riches: but the poor
hears not rebuke. The light of the righteous rejoices:
but the lamp of the wicked shall be put out.

Proverbs 13:8-9

Our lives are like lamps or lights. We have the
potential to illuminate the lives and paths around
us. Our children, spouses, friends and co-workers
have us as examples. The way we live our lives
directly impacts the amount of light we can shed on
those we love. As people who choose to live
righteously, our lights will rejoice. The presence of
righteousness will be shining for all those who are
around us. When we are faced with doing the right
things in the eyes of the Lord and choose them, our
lights are refreshed and shine in a way that is steady
and reliable.

If we desire to influence those around us, we must
be sensitive to what may seem like insignificant
moral choices. The Spirit of Truth will speak to us
and His Word will be our lamps. Let's choose
righteousness and expect our lives to help others
see.

ಬಿ Pride ಲ್

Only by pride comes contention: but with the well-advised is wisdom.

Proverbs 13:10

When we are contentious we are hard to get along with. We are easily annoyed. We tend to argue or disagree. The source of such attitudes is pride. We may have these thoughts: *"It is my way or no way," "I deserve this or that," "If they would change, I wouldn't be like this,"* etc. Contention is rooted in self-focus. Oh, that we would be people who humble ourselves under the mighty hand of God and seek to please Him! This would cause the contention to cease. The Lord says that contention comes *only* by pride — not PMS, not financial pressures, but by *pride.*

Let us come before Him now and ask for humility of mind so we won't be the contentious women who sound like a dripping faucets or the contentious men who rule from pride setting themselves up for a fall.

❧ Increase ☙

Wealth gotten by empty pursuits shall be diminished:
but he that gathers by labor shall increase.

Proverbs 13:11

Empty pursuits take effort and labor but you end up with nothing to show for it. These pursuits can be understood by looking at a helium balloon. It moves around, its presence is obvious but there really is nothing of substance. When we seek after money using empty means, the wealth we are seeking is like that balloon. It is fragile and gone in what seems like an instant. Getting things using credit only allows us to feel good in the immediate. When the items grow old, so does the thrill of the initial purchases. When the bills come, the satisfaction of what we acquired diminishes. Accruing debt to look wealthy is emptiness — no lasting substance. The Lord wants us to be people who look to and can wait upon Him to give us the desires of our hearts.

We must be hard workers who are willing to save up for things. Then we will appreciate them and teach the next generation the value of possessions. Our pursuits of any item should be marked by a willingness to work for and have the money available to purchase it. This helps us know God's will. He is our provider. If the money is not there, perhaps He does not think it a good thing at the time. He may want us to depend on Him, rather than credit to provide.

Let us stop getting wealth by emptiness. Look to the Lord to provide. Work hard. Don't give in to your fallen nature that cries out for immediate gratification. Wait on the Lord. He will renew your strength and you will be satisfied.

∞ Waiting ∞

Hope deferred makes the heart sick: but when the desire comes, it is a tree of life.

Proverbs 13:12

We have a fallen nature that always wants more and wants to get things immediately. Something within us tells us we deserve it and we deserve it now. When we have hope for something and it doesn't happen when we think it should, we can get unsettled, agitated or disturbed.

Credit is an attempt to cure this sickness of the heart. Credit tries to appease the heart's demands to have its desires immediately fulfilled. The option of stealing is another remedy for this sickness. Whining and complaining to our spouses or parents might also be another antidote for this sickness of the heart. Our fleshly natures want things and wants them immediately. The problem is that our *old man* is like a child in the store demanding the candy bar because he wants it and he wants it now. If we give in to the tantrums of a child, we nurture that attitude. If we give ourselves everything we crave, we create a self-centered, impatient and even more demanding character.

We can present our desires before the Lord who satisfies the soul of every living thing. Our Father determines when or if the desires are good for us. No good thing will He withhold from those who walk uprightly. We bring these desires before Him, trusting His wisdom and love. He is a good Father. We seek Him for wisdom and a plan if the desire is out of our reach financially. We give Him control to build our lives as He sees best. We surrender our *bratty* natures to the control of the wisdom and providence of our God. Then, if that desire is met, we find ourselves closer to Him. We end up appreciating Him and His involvement more than the fulfilled desire. Our Father reveals Himself as our Provider and the One who blesses our lives. His provision is like a tree of life. When others see how the Lord grants our desires, they have the opportunity to witness a loving Father's care for His children. Let us delight ourselves in Him, recognize when He gives us the desires of our hearts and use these times to glorify Him.

❧ Regard ☙

Whoever despises the word shall be destroyed: but he that fears the commandment shall be rewarded. The law of the wise is a fountain of life, to depart from the snares of death. Good understanding gives favor: but the way of transgressors is hard.

Proverbs 13:13-15

Our attitudes toward God's Word are the very beginning of wisdom. Do we esteem Him to be right in all matters of life? Do we allow our own understanding to be esteemed a better source of guidance than the very words of God?

Despising the Word of God is not hatred or loathing; it is an attitude of indifference and neglect. If we are given a tremendous financial gift and continue looking for provision elsewhere, we are despising this gift. The same is true for the commandments of God. The Lord has given us His judgments on life. He has preserved His Word for us to discover how to conduct ourselves and understand our existence.

When we have a high regard for His Law, we experience refreshment and springs of life. When we despise His Word, we end up with destruction. Using the Word of God to understand life, will grant us favor, and bless our relationships and pursuits. If we violate, disregard or transgress His Law, our paths becomes unnecessarily difficult and hard.

Perhaps it is a good time to stop and ask the Lord to give you a proper fear and respect for His commandments, expecting to be rewarded.

ଓ Prudence ଓ

Every prudent man deals with knowledge: but a fool lays open his foolishness.

Proverbs 13:16

A prudent person conducts themselves with knowledge. Knowledge is based on truth and not conjecture or feelings. A prudent person doesn't jump to conclusions or fill in the blanks based upon moods or triggers. We must be people who are able to deal with our spouses, children, co-workers, finances and other relationships with knowledge.

A prudent person knows the balance in their accounts and any future financial obligations. He takes into consideration a person's track record and their intentions. She gains understanding about a conflict or a child's lack of maturity to deal with the situation with knowledge. He asks questions and hopes for the best rather than labeling someone. A prudent parent searches out a matter before handing out consequences to his child that might be too harsh or too lenient.

A foolish woman displays foolishness. A foolish man speaks rashly and vents all he feels. A foolish man speaks his mind without regard for understanding and knowledge. A foolish woman tears down her home.

Lord, help us. Send us knowledge that will help us deal with things in a way that honors You and produces the decisions You want for our lives.

୫ Messengers ଓ

A wicked messenger falls into mischief: but a faithful ambassador is health.

Proverbs 13:17

Messengers are to be accurate when delivering the words or intentions of another. We are warned that if we are not faithful messengers we will find ourselves suddenly in trouble. When we repeat something to our children the other parent has said, are we accurately representing them? If we repeat a matter to a friend, are we slanting things in our favor or with some sort of mischievous intent behind it? When we don't deliver a message in its accuracy, both in content and tone, we can end up in conflict and trouble.

We will *fall* into mischief. *Falling* implies a sudden loss of footing and entrapment. We want to be faithful ambassadors — faithful to our managers, spouses, friends and the Lord. When we deliver messages, let us be slow to speak and seek to be as gracious and accurate as possible. If we are not sure about something, we should go back to the one who sent us and *then* deliver the message. Let us never fill in the blanks just to get something done. This way we can walk steadily and bring health to those who hear us. We will avoid unnecessary trouble caused by our own laziness or wickedness.

ഌ Regard ☙

Poverty and shame shall be to him that refuses instruction: but he that regards correction shall be honored.

Proverbs 13:18

When we regard correction we will be honored. To *regard correction* means we want to be shown where we are falling short or where we need to improve. Anyone who is good at anything got there by finding out what they were doing wrong. The Lord is so good. He never shows us where we are wrong without sending the instruction to teach us how to do what is right. He is a good teacher.

If parents want their children to honor them, they need to see a mom/dad who is learning, correcting, apologizing and growing. This creates an environment where the Holy Spirit is welcomed and pride and stubbornness are not. Children will honor parents who love correction. When there is humility of mind there is the grace of the Lord. The presence of the Lord will be obvious to all in our homes. His instruction will flow and homes will become more and more under His tutorship and leading.

Correction is associated with finances. If we are people who refuse instruction, financial ruin and shame will follow. If we want to be blessed financially, we need to be instructed by the Lord through whatever means He sends. Perhaps we are reaping from impulsive expenditures and accruing exorbitant interest on credit cards. We must embrace the instruction of painful consequences, learning from our mistakes.

Don't refuse instruction. Be open to His chastening and correction. He loves us and all of His discipline is rooted in a heart that loved us enough to give every last drop of blood on our behalf. He is very smart. He is the wisdom we need to conduct our lives in a way that is safe and blessed. Embrace the instruction He gives you and don't refuse it. Shame and poverty await those who refuse instruction but he that regards correction will receive honor.

❧ Fulfilled ☙

The desire accomplished is sweet to the soul: but it is abomination to fools to depart from evil.

Proverbs 13:19

When we have a desire we are often tempted to make it happen on our terms and on our schedule. We must realize that desires are often placed in our hearts by the Lord. If He puts them there, He intends to see them fulfilled. We sometimes confuse desires with goals. Goals can be clearly defined. Goals are able to be accomplished, with His help, in a very disciplined and structured manner. Desires are things we wish for. They are to be brought before the Lord in prayer. He is to be sought concerning any direction He might have for our desires. When these desires become *defined* by Him, they are *accomplished* by Him. The result is a sweet experience as we recall initially desiring them and realize who ultimately brought them to pass.

When we have a desire, we must be cautious not to try to bring it about in our own strength and on our own terms. The enemy can tempt us to use evil means to bring about something that might be noble. We will be foolish if we are hasty with our feet or words.

We must wait on the Lord concerning our desires and depart from evil strategies that might present themselves in order to see these desires fulfilled. Then, the Lord will be glorified and we will be wise people who are not controlled by the desires of our hearts.

ℰ Friends ℭ

*He that walks with wise men shall be wise: but a
companion of fools shall be destroyed.*

Proverbs 13:20

The people we hang out with affect the development
of our character. We have the ability to choose
whom we will invest time in and which relationships
we will cultivate. Each of us is given only 24 hours in
a day. This time is a gift from the Lord and we need
to seek how He would have us use it. We need to be
aware of every relationship in our lives. Is this
someone we should walk with or consider a
companion?

Although Jesus wants us to love and reach out to
everyone, we need to evaluate who should be close
companions in the light of wisdom.

> Do they fear the Lord and are they more
> concerned about pleasing Him than being
> right or comfortable?
> Do they seek God's judgment through His
> Word and wise counsel?
> Do they honor their spouses and love their
> children?
> Are they content and thankful with the
> financial situation the Lord has them in?
> Are they someone who knows it is dangerous
> to have self-confidence?
> Are they humble in their thinking and open
> to correction?
> Does this person build up their home with
> their words and attitudes?
> Do they go to work on time and are they
> reliable?
> Are they involved in patterns of sin and
> unwilling to give them up?

We will be wise if we have wise friends. One of the best things we can do in becoming wise people is choose our friends carefully. A companion of fools will be destroyed. Here are some biblical tests for foolishness.

> Are they a busybody or gossip?
> Is the person contentious and always in conflict based upon self-interest?
> Does this person tear down their house in words or choices?
> Is this person lazy?
> Does this person spend a lot of time comparing themselves with others?
> Is this person immodest and flippant in their choice of clothing and mannerisms?
> Is this person someone who does things behind their mate's back in secret?
> Does this person vent all they feel?

These are just a few questions we can ask when choosing someone to walk alongside. If you find yourself already walking with a fool, gently wean yourself from them in love. Stay committed to the person but *not* the relationship. If you do not have anyone in your life that is wise, become the wise person that someone else will want to walk with.

❦ Inheritance ❧

Evil pursues sinners: but to the righteous good shall be repaid. A good man leaves an inheritance to his children's children: and the wealth of the sinner is laid up for the just.

Proverbs 13:21-22

Choosing to walk in obedience to God leads to paths that are less complicated than the paths of sin. When we are doing things that are good and righteous, we not only enjoy our lives more, but leave an inheritance to the next generation. I have attended many funerals and find it interesting that a person's character and lifestyle are remembered *more* than belongings, achievements or notoriety. Our examples are what will affect the next generation and the one following.

As we seek the Lord to please and honor Him with our lives, the generational impact is far greater than we consider in the present. Leaving a godly heritage to our families is the most valuable inheritance. Don't ever diminish or consider a life lived for Christ as anything less than an investment with great returns. Our current choices will go into the next generation and the one after that. To the righteous, good shall be repaid. A good man leaves an inheritance to his children's children.

❧ Laziness ☙

Much food is in the tillage of the poor: but there is that which is destroyed for lack of judgment.

Proverbs 13:23

The Lord has set up a law concerning diligence and provision. As a result, the opposite holds true as well — laziness creates lack.

Even if we don't have a lot of money, if we "till" or "work diligently," we will have plenty of food. This word "tillage" means *to plow or work the land*. It is a word associated with freshly plowed land. A poor farmer who doesn't have much but faithfully tends to what he *does* have, is promised food. Freshly plowed land cannot be left to harden with the weather conditions. It is tended to *daily* in order to prepare the ground and have it ready for the seed.

We are often tempted with looking at what we don't have. A poor farmer could spend his days gazing into his empty barns or he could go out in the field and do something about it. He can patiently prepare his fields, dependent upon God and end up filling those empty barns.

Brothers and sisters, we must stop looking *beyond* the fields the Lord has given us — the advertisements, what others have, friends and family, and take care of what He has already given us. We must be people who know what is worth our time and investment and what may, in fact, be wasted concerns. If we do not tend to the land we have, it may dry up and our barns will remain empty due to our own laziness and wandering hearts.

If we lack judgment we will be destroyed, but if we take what the Lord has given us and diligently tend to it, we will not lack what we need. Take inventory of the "fields" the Lord has given you — your car, clothing, home, body etc... Are you tending to these things? Are they clean and maintained? Are things in order? Are they "freshly plowed" or neglected while you spend your time in discontentment and covetousness? Ask the Lord for judgment and discretion. Ask Him to help you know what fields He has given you and how you might be faithful in plowing them. He promises to bless your labor.

❦ Discipline ☙

He that spares his rod hates his son: but he that loves him disciplines him consistently.

Proverbs 13:24

The "rod" represents instruction and training. A rod would be used not only to strike something but as a measurement in building things. Parents can be indifferent about what their children are doing or not doing. Parents fail to pray about their roles in their children's lives. Parents need to ask Him what they could do to help lift a standard or how to administer consequences. Whenever parents are lazy, they are *not* actively loving their children. When correction is given, whether physical consequences in a controlled, non-angry way or other consequences, parents are truly loving their children.

Parents must not grow weary in well doing. In due season, they shall reap if they don't give up. Rods are to be rooted in eternal truths. Being a parent is a calling. Parents must use great restraint when administering correction. They are to conduct themselves in a worthy way. Parents are not to look through the eyes of how situations will affect *themselves*, but how they can train their children in the way *they* should go. Consistency and attentiveness to training their children results in offspring who will understand love rooted in truth and commitment.

If parents find themselves inconsistent and lazy, holding back the "rod', they must cry out to the Lord for the perseverance and consistency that He has with us. We must not believe our adversary who desires parents to back down and seek first their own kingdoms.

If the Lord has given you children, He has given you this calling. You are responsible to hold high the Lord's standard. You are to implement measures that will help your children understand consequences before they leave home and experience consequences far beyond the pain of loving discipline.

We are loved by a God who is consistent and His laws hold true. He is perfecting that which concerns us. May we know the Lord's heart toward our children and seek to reflect the same commitment and love. If you do not have children of your own, pray for those dearest to you who have such great responsibility.

❦ Content ❧

The righteous eats to the satisfying of his soul: but the belly of the wicked shall lack.

Proverbs 13:25

When we are right with God we are settled and content. We recognize and enjoy the blessings the Lord has given us. When we live wickedly our lives become so complicated we can't see beyond the mess we got ourselves in.

The Lord is good and has done so much for us. Choosing to obey Him and focus on doing what He says is right, will enable us to savor and taste that the Lord is good. Our adversary is desperately trying to blind us to the goodness of God. He wants to create in us a sense of dissatisfaction. This results in a wrong understanding of God. We might begin to see Him as thoughtless, not caring, and distant. No! The Lord God is good to His children. Deep inside of us is a hunger that only He can satisfy.

We should wake up in the morning and sit before Him, crying out to honor Him in our lives. When we do this, we have clarity. Beauty and satisfaction fill our lives.

Believers, let us *seek first* His kingdom and His righteousness, His priorities for our lives and families. We will then be satisfied and not led down the road of thirst rooted in choices He has asked us to avoid.

Lord, may we richly enjoy all good things bringing You the honor as a good Father and Shepherd of our souls.

༻ Build ༺

Every wise woman builds her house: but the foolish plucks it down with her hands.

Proverbs 14:1

There is great contrast between a wise woman and a foolish woman. The wise woman is building her house and the foolish one is plucking it down with her hands. A wise woman is not just maintaining her home *but building* it. Building implies new construction, materials, a design or plan and labor.

Women need to always look to the Master Architect for the extreme makeover He wants to do. He sees potential and problems that need repair and upgrades. Relationships in the home, priorities and attitudes are all things He loves to come in and inspect. He knows that the day-to-day living causes homes to naturally dilapidate and need His constant care and plan. The materials women need come from Him.

Women should seek Him to reveal what needs to be done. By listening to bible studies, personal times with Him and remaining sensitive to His leading throughout their days, they discover His truths to build into the structure and layout of their lives and homes. As women cooperate with Him and know, they are His laborers, they build their homes.

If you are a woman, are you seeking Him for His ideas and input for your home? Do you understand that you have a great influence on the infrastructure of your home? Do you take this seriously and look to Him for new ways to build up those who dwell within your home? Do you keep the climate of your home open to the Lord's presence and leading?

If women pluck down their homes, they are foolish women. Fools have sorrow. "Plucking" is a term that is not related to major demolition. It is like a termite slowly nibbling away at the structure. This nibbling produces hidden and devastating damage that could make the whole structure unstable and unsafe. The words women say, the thoughts they think, the choices they make, could little by little, tear down their homes. Before they know it, their families and lives will fall apart.

If you have been a foolish woman, repent and seek to be wise. Your home will withstand the elements because you are actively cooperating with the Master Builder.

❧ Consistent ☙

He that walks in his uprightness fears the LORD: but he that is twisted in his ways despises him.

Proverbs 14:2

When we fear the Lord, our steps will prove it. Those who fear the Lord are making choices and taking steps that honor Him because *His* eyes are upon them. If we think we can hide certain choices from God, we do not fear Him nor consider His presence in our lives. Our lives must be open and vulnerable to His judgments and evaluations. We must trust Him to send us His assessment of the steps we are taking.

If we do certain things in haste and try hard *not* to hear Him, we despise Him and show that we think we know better. Believers, do not allow the temptation of secret sin to diminish your perspective of our great and mighty God. He sees it all and He will deal with us as any good father would. He will discipline us and there is nothing hidden from Him. Trust Him.

Put the things that you are ashamed of in the light of His x-ray vision and allow Him to diagnose and treat the broken fellowship you have with Him. Walk consistently today knowing He is worthy to be obeyed and feared. Your life will be so much less complicated and your path so much plainer.

❧ Stubborn ☙

In the mouth of the foolish is a rod of pride: but the lips of the wise shall protect them.

Proverbs 14:3

When we speak foolishly we have *pride* at the very core of our motivation. Words can tear down a house, a marriage or a parent-child relationship. We must remember that words are very powerful. They can bring life and they can bring death. When our words are foolish, they are rooted in some sort of self-focus. When we are focused on self we are not aware of others' needs and feelings. For some reason, the rod of pride banishes the interests and feelings of others.

This rod of pride is stubborn and judgmental. It is swung with disregard to all those in its path. The Lord wants our lips to speak wise things. Wise words grace all those who hear them. Wise words are rooted in love and concern for honoring God *and* loving others. When we are wise, our words will preserve us. They will protect us from unnecessary conflict. These wise words will nurture our relationships and preserve them from decay.

When we speak words that are strong in judgment and harsh in delivery, we should stop, perhaps remove ourselves from the conversation and confess the rod of pride. Ask the Lord for humility and meekness. Wisdom is associated with meekness and consideration. When words are wise they don't have to prove themselves right. They *are* right. Lord, give us the ability to stop in the midst of foolish words and confess self-focus. Help us have a meekness that seeks to build up others and consider them more important than ourselves. In Jesus' name, amen.

ஒ Messes ஃ

Where no oxen are, the barn is clean: but much
increase is by the strength of the ox.

Proverbs 14:4

If there are no oxen in the barn, the barn is clean.
There is no hay to be stored, no flies associated with
their presence, no waste on the ground and the dirt
doesn't get disturbed — it's a smooth, clean surface
to walk in and admire. Having a clean barn is not
supposed to be the goal of someone who owns a
barn. If we were to visit a farmer/cattle rancher and
find his facilities sparkling clean and quiet without
traces of livestock, we would wonder what sort of
farmer he is. We would wonder how he plows his
fields or gathers his harvest. We would question his
success and identity. Although things would look
nice, they would seem strange and the barn would
not only be empty of messes, but the grain itself
would be missing or minimal.

Brethren, we have been given facilities by the Lord —
our homes, cars, and material goods. Sometimes in
seeking to take care of our goods and keep our
homes in order, we can miss His purposes in giving
them to us. Our *oxen* are often *people* who can
create messes. This results in extra work for us.
Spouses, roommates, friends and family fill our lives
and homes. As a result, things aren't always as clean
as we might like them to be. But...there *is* much
increase through the strength of the ox.

The people in our lives are placed there by the Lord
to bring about an increase in our lives, to plow and
harvest all the Lord wants to grow in us. When we
have messes as a result of our children or having
others in our homes, we must remember God's truth

more than fleshly perspectives. We are supposed to work willingly with our hands, welcome messes as a result of relationships and thank Him for all He is doing in our lives through those around us.

ஐ Truth ﳗ

A faithful witness will not lie: but a false witness will utter lies.

Proverbs 14:5

Truth is the mark of integrity. We are His witnesses and it is important we are people who seek to be honest and accurate in all our dealings. To every man is given a measure of faith. People's faith should be guarded and their hearts handled with great care. Truth, no matter how difficult it may be, is something that can be faced and dealt with. Lies create mistrust and confusion.

If there is a truth we sense another is not ready for, we are not forced to lie. We explain to them that we don't feel it is the right time to give them that information. That is still speaking the truth. The devil is the father of *all* lies and we don't want him to birth anything in our lives. If you sense the Spirit of Truth bringing to mind someone you lied to, ask Him how you might get things right. Parents should consider what they are telling their children concerning legends and holiday traditions. We want to be faithful witnesses.

৪০ Clarity ০৪

A scorner seeks wisdom, and finds it not: but knowledge is easy to him that understands.

Proverbs 14:6

In this life we need wisdom and knowledge to make good decisions when faced with situations that demand our response.

A scorner is one who looks down on others. If we find ourselves talking down to anyone, we won't be able to hear the facts and might contribute to the problem.

At work we may find ourselves emotionally involved with an injustice and tempted to react sarcastically or with a high-minded attitude. We won't find the knowledge or wisdom to address the matter when we are in this mindset.

In our marriages we may find ourselves frustrated with some sort of impasse. In order to get the understanding and knowledge we need to resolve this, we must cast out the scorner within us. We must humble ourselves and seek God to show us *our* responsibilities without focusing on others' faults.

The word "understand" is made up of two words — "under" and "stand'. We must place ourselves in a *standing* position *under* the situation. We have to be able to gain perspective on a problem by removing ourselves from the emotional side and looking beneath the surface. If we are mocking or scorning, we will not find His answers. The next time we are in a situation where we need understanding, let's not react emotionally. Let's stop and ask the Lord for understanding. Then we will find ourselves equipped with the knowledge and tools to handle the matter.

ଚ Leave ଓ

*Go from the presence of a foolish man, when you do
not perceive in him the lips of knowledge. The wisdom
of the prudent is to understand his way: but the
foolishness of fools is deceit. Fools make a mock at
sin: but among the righteous there is favor.*

Proverbs 14:7-9

We are not to remain in the presence of someone
who is speaking foolishly. If we are around those
who are deceived or are comfortable with deceiving
others, we are not in a good place. These friendships
will contribute to confusion and cloud our ability to
understand our way. Deception can cross over and
darken the plainness of the path of the righteous.
Wise friends will help us seek the Lord and
understand what the Lord wants us to do. We need
the Lord to give us wisdom in choosing companions
as well as how to conduct ourselves in social
settings. If we find ourselves in the presence of
someone speaking foolishly, we are advised to seek
an appropriate escape from the conversation.

A foolish person mocks sin. We can hear people on
television or radio laugh at sinful situations. We can
be in a conversation where sinful actions are the
center of a joke. At that point, we should change the
station or leave the presence of such dialogue. We
need righteous companionship — friends who
promote favor with God. We need people in our
lives who seek to please God and do what He deems
right.

Leave the presence of a foolish person when you do
not perceive the lips of knowledge. This will protect
you and establish your life. You will not leave the
path the Lord has for you but rather maintain a

steady course without needless detours and tragedies. You will be delivered from your adversary's traps.

ℰ Deep ℭ

The heart knows his own bitterness; and a stranger will not meddle with his joy.

Proverbs 14:10

What is deep within us is *deep* within us. Our hearts have feelings and experiences that no one is able to connect with on a human level. When we go through things we often realize that no matter how much someone loves us they cannot be the companion we need in our hearts. If we are having bitterness or sorrow, we wish someone could come in and help us carry the weight. We can find ourselves feeling isolated from and disappointed with those who surround us.

When we have joy and excitement deep within our souls, we can find ourselves amazed that others don't join us with the same joy and passion we are experiencing. Our hearts know our *own* bitterness and a stranger does not get involved in *our* heart's joy. This is only found in someone who can come *into* our hearts and experience highs and lows with us. That's Jesus Christ!

In Ephesians 3:17, Paul prays for the believers, *"That Christ may dwell in your hearts by faith; that, being rooted and grounded in love..."* Now, we have Christ in our hearts and His presence will make a difference.

He is in our hearts and is able to:

- Have His peace rule and reign in our hearts when they are troubled.
  Col 3:15 *And let the peace of God rule in your hearts, to which you are called in one body; and be thankful.*
- Comfort our hearts when they are hurting.

2 Thess 2:16-17 *Now our Lord Jesus Christ himself, and God, even our Father, which has loved us, and has given us everlasting comfort and good hope through grace, Comfort your hearts , and establish you in every good word and work.*

- Direct our hearts into His love when others might not be loving us.
  2 Thess 3:5 *And the Lord direct your hearts into the love of God, and into the patient waiting for Christ.*
- Search our hearts when we are confused.
  Acts 1:24 *And they prayed, and said, You, Lord, which knows the hearts of all men*

We must not allow ourselves to place expectations on human relationships that only the presence of the Lord Jesus can consistently meet as well as exceed.

ஐ Climate ෬

The house of the wicked shall be overthrown: but the
tabernacle of the upright shall flourish.

Proverbs 14:11

The climate of our homes are directly impacted by
how we are living. If we are people who are walking
uprightly we are contributing to a flourishing
environment for our children, mates, and those who
live with us. We help nurture and maintain a place
where people feel safe and are not caught by
surprise because of secret sins or hidden
compromise. Our homes will flourish and we will
benefit from it. Others in our homes might be doing
wickedly and will definitely impact our homes, but,
if we focus on living for the Lord, the destruction
will be met with life. Do you desire to have a rich
and fruitful dwelling place? Take heed to yourself
first and watch the trickle-effect your devotion to
Christ will have on all those living with you.

ও Perspective ং

There is a way which seems right to a man, but the end of that way are the ways of death.

Proverbs 14:12

We must not be people who trust our own judgment. Things can seem one way but be cloaked with a deceptive covering. In the Garden of Eden, Eve looked at the forbidden fruit and evaluated whether she should eat it. She concluded it seemed right to her. In humility of mind, we must seek the Lord and acknowledge Him in all of our ways so He might direct our paths. We may be influenced by all kinds of things that distort our discretion and judgment.

The Lord does not necessarily call us to go in a way that *seems* right to us. He calls us to go in the way that *is* right for us. The beginning of a road that seems right might have as its ultimate destination — death. He is the God who is and was and is to come. He knows where steps in a certain direction will take us. We must trust His ability and love to guide our lives. Just because something appears good, does not make it good.

ও Pain ଔ

Even in laughter the heart is sorrowful; and the end of that mirth is heaviness.

Proverbs 14:13

Oftentimes we see people looking like they are having a good time. These people may be in a restaurant we visit, in line behind us at a store or next to us in our workplaces. This appearance can trick us into thinking that they are happy and content.

The Lord warns us that even when someone is laughing, their heart may, in fact, be *full* of sorrow. Sometimes people even laugh harder to cover up pain and sorrow. When we are around people, believers or non-believers, we need to remain observant and sensitive to their hearts. We need to listen to the Holy Spirit if He illuminates someone in the room and draws our hearts toward them. We cannot take laughter at face value. Listen to their words for hints of some sort of pain or sorrow. The Lord might want to use us to minister to them. We are not to actively seek out pain in others, but rather not go along with the climate of a conversation without being aware of pain or burdens.

The next time everyone is laughing, let's remember that someone in that group could be full of sorrow and heaviness. Let's not allow group dynamics to camouflage the needs of the individual.

✥ Upward ✥

The backslider in heart shall be filled with his own ways: and a good man shall be satisfied from himself.

Proverbs 14:14

It is interesting to note that the Lord is dealing with backslidings in *heart*. Our hearts represent our focus and affection. To protect ourselves from being filled with our own ways of backsliding, we must be sure that our hearts are going toward the upward call of God in Christ. Our affections must be set on the things above and our value systems should reflect the worth of eternal pursuits and judgments. In our hearts, we must hide His Word and we must be making a melody to Him. This will protect us from sliding back, in our hearts.

If we were to be roller skating up a hill we would slide back under two conditions:

If we were not skating upward, leaning into the hill

-or-

Standing passively on the incline not moving at all.

We need to be people who are ascending the hill of the Lord. We need to be people who lean into the ascent. This approach not only prevents us from sliding back, but lends itself to progress and growth.

Believers, let us be people who seek first the kingdom of God and His righteousness knowing that, if we set Him before us, we will always be heading in the right direction.

❧ Think ☙

The simple believes every word: but the prudent man looks well to his going.

Proverbs 14:15

When we are receiving information we would be wise to exercise caution. We would do well to develop our critical thinking skills.

When others come to us with their side of the story or a co-worker explains a problem, we should be *loving enough* to listen and care, yet wise enough to search out the matter. We need to discover the most accurate portrayal of their difficulties.

Everyone has filters and perspectives that affect their perception. If we are going to be wise, we must take these things into account being sensitive to any missing or emotionally distorted facts. The Lord is truth and He will help us grow in our ability to look well to our goings.

Even reading a devotional like this, or a Christian book, should involve a certain amount of caution, not believing every word. If we do this, our paths will be much clearer and built on truth rather than the course of man's words and conclusions.

❧ Careful ☙

A wise man fears, and departs from evil: but the fool rages, and is confident.

Proverbs 14:16

We need to be sensitive to the fact that we do *not* obey the Lord *naturally*. We *naturally* go our *own* ways. This should produce in us a fear — hesitancy and caution when dealing with our natural responses.

We have the opportunity to destroy and tear down all the Lord is building in our lives. This should cause us to take intentional steps and have a spiritual ear inclined to His voice. If we are people who operate in brazen self-confidence we set ourselves up for unnecessary destruction.

There *will be* snares and traps our adversary will put before us *today*. When we fear the Lord, we depart from evil. May we be people who renounce self-confidence and humbly walk in the fear of the Lord,

‮ಐ‬ Anger ಐ

He that is soon angry deals foolishly: and a man of wicked devices is hated.

Proverbs 14:17

God is so good to define "foolishness". This helps us move away from foolishness and toward the new man which is created in true righteousness and holiness.

If we are people who are easily angered, we deal foolishly. A variety of factors could affect our disposition. If we are tired, stressed or emotional, our fuses could be running a little short. It would be wise to avoid situations that could ignite these short fuses. We must not make provision for the flesh to fulfill its lusts. When we are not in a good state of mind, we should be on guard with our first responses.

For *every* temptation there is a way of escape. As soon as we find ourselves becoming angered or annoyed, we should confess this and seek the Lord to show us the way of escape. These attitudes are not acceptable and misrepresent God who is not easily angered. Moses was not allowed to enter into the Promised Land because his anger got in the way and resulted in misrepresenting the Lord. We must seek the Lord for His patient love. Let's cry out to Him asking Him to fill us with this slow-to-anger love. We should ask Him how to avoid factors that could be contributing to our short tempers. When we do lose our tempers, we should always apologize to the Lord and anyone affected by it. Let us not miss entering into the land that the Lord has promised us.

ᛒ Ignorance ᛜ

The simple inherit foolishness: but the prudent are crowned with knowledge.

Proverbs 14:18

The Lord doesn't want us to be simple people. This word "simple" means, not knowing anything. It is an ignorance associated with apathy and laziness. A simple person just exists and allows life, feelings and circumstances to blow them in any given direction at any given time. This kind of person will inherit foolishness. They will make foolish decisions and reap horrible consequences. In order to cope with the myriad of situations they have fallen into, they might turn to alcohol or drugs to numb themselves.

The Lord wants His people to be crowned with knowledge. Knowledge and understanding help us wear the crown of lordship over the events and circumstances that blow into our lives. We become the ones who can *decide* what to do in situations rather than have *them* redirect our lives. If we are wearing the crown of knowledge, we will make decisions that are guided by the Lord and our lives will reveal what a wise and holy God we serve.

Let us not sit back and inherit foolishness through aimless existences but rather wake up in our inner man *seeking* the Lord for His judgment on matters. Let us make choices with His wisdom He promises to give liberally. If we lack some sort of life skill, let's rejoice that Jesus is the life and will give us everything pertaining to life and godliness. Let's rejoice that He is our Teacher in *all* things and He will crown us with knowledge.

ઝ Observe ભ

The evil bow before the good; and the wicked at the gates of the righteous.

Proverbs 14:19

Sometimes when people are directly disobeying their Creator's laws of life, they seem happy and successful. We can even start to wonder whether keeping God's Word really makes a difference. This verse reveals what eventually happens. The evil will bow before the good and the wicked bow at the gates of the righteous. In Psalm 73, David started to be hypnotized and deceived by the apparent success of evildoers. Their lives appeared to be free from trouble and prosperous.

"For I was envious at the foolish, when I <u>saw</u> the prosperity of the wicked. For there are no bands in their death: but their strength is firm. They are not in trouble as other men; neither are they plagued like other men." (Ps 73:3-5)

David was going by what he *saw* and his conclusions led him to envy. The wicked *seemed* to be getting away with everything and enjoying life to the fullest.

What we *see* and what is *really* happening in the hearts of men, are often very far apart. People present themselves in their best light on social media. When we meet up for the holidays, everyone is dressed their best, and presenting their polished presence. In Psalm 73 we learn David was in a *slippery place* and full of unnecessary pain by observing others. He was coming to the wrong conclusions based on what he *saw* and what he *thought*. We are in a good place when we focus on obeying our Maker and *doing* what is right in *His* sight rather than observing and analyzing *others*. In the long run we will remain standing no matter how high and lifted up others seem to be. In the same psalm the Lord tells us the wicked are in slippery places and what may appear as success can be over in just a moment.

"When I thought to know this, it was too painful for me; until I went into the sanctuary of God; then I understood their end. Surely you set them in slippery places: you cast them down into destruction. How they are brought into desolation, as in a moment! They are utterly consumed with terrors." (Ps 73:16 - 19)

Once David went into the sanctuary of God, *then* he understood how things were going to end up. We need to come into His presence and bring our observations before Him. Our evaluations could very well be rooted in partial truths and be used by our adversary to cause us to question God's goodness and truth. Ps 37:3 says, *"Trust in the LORD, and do good; so you will dwell in the land, and truly be fed."*

⁊ Favoritism ⅋

The poor is hated by his own neighbor: but the rich has many friends. He that despises his neighbor sins: but he that has mercy on the poor, happy is he.

Proverbs 14:20-21

Despising someone due to their economic worth is sin. We must never esteem someone who has money as better than those who do not. Sometimes we can favor the rich because of an apparent lack of troubles or the benefits we could gain from them. This is sin. Our value of people should come from God's standard of value and worth. They have been made by Him and for Him. Every human being is to be valued — in the womb, on the streets, in the mansion and in the mental hospital. Our hearts must beat with a desire to love and treat others with consistent respect and mercy. We will be happy when we can love and enjoy everyone around us. The Lord warns us about this tendency to favor the rich in the New Testament:

My brothers, do not believe in the Lord Jesus Christ, the Lord of glory, with certain prejudices toward different classes of people. For if there comes to your assembly a man with a gold ring, in expensive clothing, and there comes in also a poor man in dirty clothing; And you show favoritism to him that wears the expensive clothing, and say to him, Sit here in a good place; and say to the poor, Stand there, or sit here under my footstool: doesn't this reveal a divided heart and you have become someone with evil thoughts? (James 2:1-4)

We don't want to be *divided* in ourselves. We want our lives to be consistent sources of support and love to everyone we meet. In our society, status can creep into our value systems unnoticed. We should take heed to these warnings and ask God to help us value others based on their worth in His eyes and no other criteria.

❧ Good ☙

Do they not err that devise evil? But mercy and truth shall be to them that devise good.

Proverbs 14:22

God has given us creative minds. We can devise and think up many things. Because of sin, our minds can be used to think up evil plans and schemes. Many a mind have conjured up thoughts of getting even. Lustful minds have planned out sexual exploits and fantasies. Covetous minds have pictured the riches and successes that one deserves creating discontentment and jealousy. Embittered minds have entertained wicked calamities falling on those who have wounded them.

The Lord warns us we will err if we are people who use our minds to devise evil. He also tells us our lives will be blessed is we use them to devise good.

He has designed our ability to be creative for His purposes. God can speak to us in our minds with solutions and resources to meet others' needs. He can give us ideas to bless others. We can ponder what we can do for His glory and allow our minds to travel down the road of good ideas.

In order to keep our minds from devising evil, we can change our thoughts to dialogue. What were once random thoughts can be intentionally spoken to the Lord. When we take our thoughts captive to the Lord Jesus, our thoughts must obey Him. He is able to order them in the directions He would have them go. We often have little power to make our thoughts obey but when we think to the Lord, He can silence them, refine them or develop them.

People who mull over how they might reach those who do not know Christ, receive creative strategies in bringing the truth to them. Parents who prayerfully consider how to best raise their children, begin to come up with ideas and insight into their parenting skills.

Believers, the Lord has given us minds that were designed to love Him. Our creative imaginations, when brought under His control, can be used to bring about His will. If we find ourselves devising evil — we must stop! We should confess such thoughts as sin and ask Him to protect us from error. Let's redirect our thoughts and say something like, *"Lord Jesus, maybe You would have me do this,"* or *"Jesus, I could bring in more money this way."* As we begin to take our thoughts captive to His obedience, our creativity will serve as a wonderful place in which to receive the plans He has for us — plans for good, not evil, to give us a future and a hope.

ꙮ Talking ꙮ

*In all labor there is profit: but the talk of the lips
tends only to poverty.*

Proverbs 14:23

People that have the gift of gab are quite the
blessing at times. This is a great relationship builder.
The problem is that sometimes lips are talking when
hands should be working. Parents might stand
outside their children's school gabbing away, when
they should be at the market getting things for
dinner that night. People might be texting or on
social media when household tasks need to be done.
Employees might be catching up on the latest news
ignoring their responsibilities.

People often think that talking about what needs to
be done is tantamount to getting things done. If we
talk about what needs to be done rather than do
what needs to be done, we might end up in poverty.
This poverty might mean a day with nothing to
show for it or even a lifetime of struggles and empty
handedness.

The Lord gives us a great promise in this verse. He
tells us in *all* labor there is profit. If we just rinse
that *dish* or wipe down that counter, we are already
ahead. If we get out our calendars and plan that
activity we are moving in the right direction. We
might feel if a task can't be done to a certain
standard, it isn't worth starting at all.

Our sense of satisfaction in what we do is not
outcome based — but in the labor itself. If we do any
sort of labor, there is profit.

ஐ Finances ௰

The crown of the wise is their riches: but the foolishness of fools is foolishness.

Proverbs 14:24

Wisdom helps us financially. Wisdom tells us when to work and when to rest. Wisdom tells us when to save and when to spend. Wisdom tells us how much sleep we need to be effective employees. There is a correlation between walking in wisdom and financial integrity.

It is foolish to spend recklessly. Foolishness tells the employee that the expectations of their employer are unreasonable. Foolishness encourages impulsive purchases. Foolishness tells us to spend because we deserve it. Foolishness tells us to accumulate things to make us feel like we are worth something. Foolishness tells us to put off the tasks that *need* to be done and do the things we *want* to do.

Let us be sensitive to the voice of wisdom and shun the voice of foolishness. This will help us shine at work, keep our finances in order and enjoy the riches wisdom brings.

✜ Accuracy ✜

A true witness delivers souls: but a deceitful witness speaks lies.

Proverbs 14:25

Our accounts of any given situation must be as accurate as possible. We must be careful when repeating a matter or giving details that we don't slant the facts to deceive. This is not *exaggeration* or *leaving something out*. The Lord calls it *lying*. Lying is sin and sin brings about death. We must be true witnesses that will be used to deliver souls.

People have believed lies about themselves, others or God. Lies can damage people. Their souls are held captive by lies they have believed. When we speak God's truth and when we are gentle with accurate words, we will be used by the Lord to deliver people from destructive deceptions. The only way to be this true witness is to be people who graze in the truth of God's Word. When we stay in His Word and have His Word dwell in us, we will be sources of truth and deliverance. Others will hear the truth in the face of the myriad of lies their bodies, media and ungodly counsel are telling them. They will be rescued and delivered from false roads that end in destruction and despair.

We will be delivered from the lie that success is defined by our positions and possessions. We will walk with our heads up knowing we are loved and respected for our character and integrity. We will be delivered from thinking our worth is based on numbers on a scale or how few wrinkles we have. Our friends will be safe in friendships that hold no surprises and are steeped in truth and godly counsel. We will deliver our *own* souls from deceptive voices by speaking truth in *our* hearts.

Let's stay close to God's heart and word in defining truth so we will be true witnesses delivering souls that surround us.

❧ Approval ☙

In the fear of the LORD is strong confidence: and his children shall have a place of refuge. The fear of the LORD is a fountain of life, to depart from the snares of death.

Proverbs 14:26-27

The fear of the Lord enables us to be confident people. When we are tuned in to pleasing Him and Him alone, our lives are ordered. We are not controlled by the expectations of others. We will not be swayed by others' approval or disapproval.

When parents have the fear of the Lord, their children will be safe. Parenting will be rooted in eternal truths rather than moods and cultural shifts. Children need a place of refuge. The truths parents base their decisions on, will follow their children throughout their lives. The fear of the Lord will produce a fountain of life. If parents build their lives on the fear of anything or anyone else they will create an unstable environment. Children will be pulled into a tumultuous existence they will find difficult to navigate.

As we are concerned about His evaluation of our days, there will be new avenues of refreshing direction in our lives. We will avoid snares that our adversary has set for us, finding refuge and safety for us and our children. Oh Lord that we would be people whose confidence comes from fearing You alone.

ℬ Leadership ℭ

*In the multitude of people is the king's honor: but in
the lack of people is the destruction of the prince.*

Proverbs 14:28

Many people under a king's rule often shows a
stability of the kingdom and implies people feel safe
and comfortable under his leadership.

When there is a lack of people following a leader it
may be evidence that the leader is not the kind of
leader people want to follow.

If we are given a leadership position we must
remember that Jesus has clearly instructed His
followers to lead as servants. Any good coach knows
that wins come from the players on the field and not
the coach himself. The players need instruction,
encouragement and correction. They are to be
invested in.

Whether at work, in ministry or at home, when we
are given a leadership position we must remember
that it is really all about those we are leading and
not the position itself. Honor comes from serving
those we lead. People stay under good leadership.
When a leader has consistent followers, this may be
the mark of an effective leader.

ॐ Meek ॐ

He that is slow to wrath is of great understanding:
but he that is hasty of spirit exalts foolishness.

Proverbs 14:29

We should be people who are slow to anger and not
hasty in our spirits. Our inner man should be meek
and quiet, which in the sight of God is of great
worth. This takes discipline in pondering and
cherishing within our hearts. God's people are to
have fellowship in the inner man with the Lord Jesus
Christ. By letting the Word of Christ dwell richly
within us, we will open our mouths and be able to
teach and admonish others rather than spill forth
hateful and wrathful words. The heart is to be
maintained. Our inner man is to be making melody
to the Lord. As we have fellowship with Him we
won't be hasty in spirit. Our reactions will be guided
by the Lord's leading as opposed to being triggered
by circumstances or environments. It is important to
be aware of our inner man throughout the day and
let the peace of God rule our hearts and minds.

If we are hasty of spirit we will be exalting
foolishness. This means that we will most likely say,
do or encourage something foolish. A foolish woman
tears down her house with her *own* hands. A foolish
man is unreasonable and often given to wrath. Our
spirits must not be hasty but steadfastly settled in
His grace and presence.

❧ Envy ☙

A sound heart is the life of the flesh: but envy the rottenness of the bones.

Proverbs 14:30

God wants us to have a sound heart. A sound heart rests in God's goodness, producing life. When we have a sound hearts, we will be content and enjoy quality of life. A sound heart is in fellowship with God, thanking Him for all He is and does.

When we are stirred up to look at another's lot in life with envy, our frames begin to suffer structural damage. Envy is rottenness to our bones. If our bone structures were weakened through some sort of disease, we would be susceptible to fractures and not be able to take the natural bumps and bruises of day-to-day life. In the same way, when we become envious, little offenses can come in and break us down. We will not function well and end up with fractured relationships and an inability to walk uprightly.

When envy comes in, all of our relationships suffer. We can't seem to enjoy anything. But a heart that is sound will help us function in a healthy way. The remedy for envy is gratefulness for all we have and all God has done. Let us pursue soundness of heart by considering all He has given us and watch our lives suddenly become rich and full.

ஐ Poverty ௰

He that oppresses the poor reproaches his Maker: but he that honors him has mercy on the poor.

Proverbs 14:31

There are people who take advantage of the poor for their own gain. There are many liquor stores in depressed areas knowing that the plight of poverty has driven many to drown their sorrows in intoxicating drink. Drug dealers hoping to attract new addicts infiltrate the impoverished streets of certain areas knowing that a quick fix or quick money will be attractive to those who have financial pressures. Yet, in these areas, we find Christian ministry. There are food banks and soup kitchens seeking to bring relief and aid to those who struggle.

When we seek to help those who are hurting we have mercy on the poor. The Word of God tells us in Proverbs 11:17 that, *"The merciful man does good to his own soul..."* We are to consider the poor and not be consumed with seeking our own comfort. We shouldn't turn a blind eye to those who are in situations of great discomfort, whether by their own fault or circumstances beyond their control. Perhaps we will have an opportunity to show mercy and do good to our own souls.

ঙ Death ଓ

The wicked is driven away in his wickedness: but the righteous has hope in his death.

Proverbs 14:32

Death is one of those things that, if you are reading this right now, you have not experienced. We do what we can to postpone our appointments with death as long as we can. We do need to be reassured, that if we have received Christ, we are no longer in bondage to the fear of death. We have been declared righteous because His righteousness is now our clothing.

He who knew no sin became sin for us that we might become the righteousness of God in Him. We don't have to look at death as the end or a hopeless experience. Death has now been chosen as an usher to take us to be with Him forever. We don't have to like the usher or the door through which we will travel, but we can have hope that we will be with Him forever. The Lord tells us in 1 Corinthians 15:54-55 that:

"Death is swallowed up in victory. O death, where is your sting? O grave, where is your victory?"

We don't need to look hopelessly to this future appointment. We can look at death square in its eyes, clothed in the righteousness of Christ and have hope even until the end.

❧ Restlessness ☙

Wisdom rests in the heart of him that has understanding: but that which is in the midst of fools is made known.

Proverbs 14:33

When we know the wisest thing to do, we don't always need to speak it. Wisdom can rest in our hearts and manifest in our lives in a timing that proves it to be right. Foolishness is made known as well. Foolish choices often demand to be seen and noticed. Wisdom can rest in our hearts and doesn't demand the affirmation of others.

If we are in the midst of foolish counsel and input, we would do well to quiet our inner spirits and rest in the wisdom we are sure is right. This wisdom will prove itself to be enduring and produce the fruit we can enjoy. Let's not panic and determine to show how right we are and perhaps how foolish others are. We should wait on the Lord. He will strengthen our hearts and His wisdom will prove itself in time.

ಲ Reproach ಣ

Righteousness exalts a nation: but sin is a reproach to any people.

Proverbs 14:34

A nation is made up of individuals. A family is made up of individuals. The stability of a structure is established by the integrity of the components within it. When individuals seek to live lives that please the Lord, the righteousness will exalt whatever entity they find themselves a part of. To change the direction of a nation, the individuals must change direction. When members of a family begin to follow the Lord, the entire family will begin to rise above the common statistics. Before we complain about our *families* or *marriages*, let us fight for *each* member with spiritual weapons.

"...Do not be afraid of them: remember the Lord, which is great and worthy to be feared, and fight for your family, your sons, and your daughters, your wives, and your houses." (Neh 4:14)

ೞ Servantsೞ

The king's favor is toward a wise servant: but his wrath is against him that causes shame.

Proverbs 14:35

Wisdom will help us find favor in authority's eyes. When we handle life with wisdom we make those over us look good and help them avoid having to clean up foolish messes we might make. Whether it is our spouses, a principal, a manager, landlord or ministry leader, we will find favor in their eyes if we are wise people. We will make good use of our time, be punctual, take care of our properties, and follow through on any directives. If we want to have a good relationship with anyone who is in authority over us, we need to ask the Lord for wisdom and walk in it.

Consider a person's children. When they walk in wisdom don't the parents want to give them more freedom and privileges? When they are foolish or rebellious, don't parents find themselves upset and having to implement consequences? Let's remind our children or those whom we oversee of the joy they bring us when they walk in wisdom and let's do the same to bless those who oversee us.

ᛒ Responses ᚲ

A soft answer turns away wrath: but grievous words stir up anger. The tongue of the wise uses knowledge correctly: but the mouth of fools pours out foolishness.

Proverbs 15:1-2

Our verbal responses will directly influence the course of a conversation. If we have a soft answer in the midst of anger we can actually *turn away* wrath. A soft answer is soft in tone *and* content. It is not using push-button words or tones that would incite or fuel the volatile climate we might find ourselves in.

When our spouses, friends, co-workers or children come at us with wrath, we must ask the Lord for His grace to respond softly. Be quick to listen, slow to speak and slow to wrath. Listen to what the wrath might be speaking. Is the child sick? Is your husband tired? Is your wife emotionally vulnerable at the moment? Is your friend under some sort of financial pressure? Seek to have a soft answer. If you answer back with harsh words it only gets worse and the wrath of man does not work the righteousness of God.

To be the wise believers that the Lord wants us to be, we must understand the impact of our words and tones. Mouths of fools pour out foolishness. When our tongues pour out words rooted in pride, anger or self-righteousness, we are foolish. When we tell other people everything we know, we are not using knowledge correctly. The Lord would have us use knowledge for His glory, displaying His wisdom. The words of a foolish person are grievous and pour out with little or no restraint. The tongue of the wise is soft in tone and content. The tongue of the wise uses knowledge correctly and is under the control of the Holy Spirit.

Lord, help us be people whose mouths are under Your control.

ꙮ Beholding ꙮ

The eyes of the LORD are in every place, beholding the evil and the good.

Proverbs 15:3

It is so good to know the eyes of the Lord are in every place. Sometimes children are taught the Lord sees the bad things they do. The Lord beholds the good as well. When we do the right things when no one is looking, the Lord is beholding, taking notice, of what we are doing. It is important to understand that what we do in secret will be rewarded in the open. If we feel alone or unnoticed, we can be comforted by this promise. If we feel victimized by an act no one took note of, we can consider this promise. We are seen and He has seen all that has gone on in our lives — the evil *and* the *good*.

ℬ Fruit ℭ

A wholesome tongue is a tree of life: but a twisted tongue is a breach in the spirit.

Proverbs 15:4

If our mouths bring forth wholesome words we will produce a tree of life. There will be shade for our children to be covered by, fruit for our mates and friends to be nurtured by and blossoms that will bring forth the fragrance of His presence. If we cuss, gossip, deceive or speak hateful words, we produce weeds and thorns that create an ugly environment where growth is stunted. We need the Lord to train our tongues to speak words that are wholesome — words that can be treasured and produce safety for those around us. If our words are perverse, twisted in some sort of way, the spirits of those affected will be broken and weakened.

Lord, we give You our tongues. We present this little member of our bodies and ask that they be used by You to be a trees of life. Lord, show us by Your Holy Spirit when our words are perverse. Help us be sensitive to Your conviction and train us up to be the covering and fruit-bearing people You desire us to be. In Jesus' name. Amen.

ಬ Structure ಚಿ

A fool despises his father's instruction: but he that regards correction is prudent.

Proverbs 15:5

The parental authority structure is designed by God for good. Even if our earthly fathers do not follow the Lord, they still have experiences we can learn from. In order for children to give honor, parents should model that same honor to their parents regardless of their age.

Our parents have been down the road and it would be wise for us to consider their counsel on matters. We must bring their advice before the Lord and evaluate it in light of His Word. We should still regard our parents' correction. We should carefully consider their instruction and correction and see whether the Lord is speaking to us through them. To be wise requires being teachable and able to be corrected. This attribute is so rare that truly our worth will be more valuable than rubies. The next time we hear some input from our earthly parents, let's be open to instruction and correction. Even as adults, the Lord will use our parents to speak wisdom and counsel to us. This example will instruct our children how to respond when they hear *our* instruction.

⁖ Revenue ⁃

In the house of the righteous is much treasure: but in the revenues of the wicked is trouble.

Proverbs 15:6

When we are seeking to do what is right and pleasing in the eyes of the Lord, our lives and homes are filled with treasures. Treasures are things of value and not common.

When we are people who seek the Lord for His priorities, we will find our days filled with precious and pleasant substance. These treasures often elude others who are coming up with emptiness amidst all of their self-centered pursuits. We will have peace and consistency that we will value and draw from in our day-to-day existence. There will be a strength and value that might even surprise us at times.

This is not true if we choose to build our homes upon any sort of wicked scheme. The Lord promises trouble in our homes if we are people like that. Choosing the right things to do in the sight of the Lord will help us avoid unnecessary trouble and bless us with a quality of life we could never have imagined.

✌ Yielding ☙

The lips of the wise disperse knowledge: but the heart of the foolish does not so.

Proverbs 15:7

Out of the abundance of our hearts come our words. In order to have the lips of the wise, our hearts need to reject foolishness. We have read much about the fool. A fool is wise in his own eyes. Our hearts must not be like this. Our hearts need to be teachable and quiet, listening for our Lord's judgment on matters. A fool is contentious. Our hearts must not argue and fight for their own way but be yielding and submissive to the leading of the Holy Spirit. A fool tears down those who are around them. Our hearts must consider and think on the things that are worthy of praise in others. When our hearts are rooted in wisdom, our lips will give out knowledge. When we disperse knowledge, we will contribute to others' well-being. We need to be people who open our mouths with wisdom and that begins with a heart that rejects foolish patterns.

ဆ Acknowledge ☜

The sacrifice of the wicked is an abomination to the LORD: but the prayer of the upright is his delight. The way of the wicked is an abomination to the LORD: but he loves him that follows after righteousness.

Proverbs 15:8-9

There are things that are abominations to the Lord and things that bring Him delight. The sacrifice of the wicked is an abomination to the Lord. The Lord does not desire sacrifice; He desires obedience in the first place.

When we find ourselves compromising, we can be tempted to compensate by punishing ourselves or doing some sort of penance. This is not what pleases the Lord. The prayer of the upright is His delight.

He wants us to come to Him and confess our sins. He wants us to confess and forsake these ways. He doesn't want us to come up with a plan to have our good outweigh our bad. This is a wicked way.

He wants us to follow hard after righteousness and when and if we fall, to pray and call upon Him for His forgiveness and enabling. He delights in this sort of uprightness — acknowledging sin, walking before Him in His light and allowing Him to search and correct us. He loves the one who follows after righteousness and seeks to be instructed in His ways.

Let's not go about establishing our own ways of dealing with wickedness. Let's remember the sacrifice of Jesus is the only sacrifice that appeases the heart of God on our behalf. Let's come and speak to the Rock. Let's receive the cleansing and refreshment that pours forth from the One who has been smitten on our behalf. Let's follow after our

226

Righteousness and enjoy the fellowship and access
He has paid for at such a high price.

➳ Heart ᘄ

Correction is grievous to him that forsakes the way: and he that hates correction shall die. Hell and destruction are before the LORD: how much more, the hearts of the children of men? A scorner doesn't love the one that corrects him: neither will he go to the wise.

Proverbs 15:10 -12

Our hearts are open before the Lord and He is the best heart surgeon we could want. Correction is absolutely necessary to maintain a healthy heart. A heart open to correction is the heart the Lord wants us to have. Our hearts can be hardened by the deceitfulness of sin. We should submit ourselves to the Surgeon's instrument, the sword of the Spirit — the Word of God.

The Lord wants to examine our hearts. We should be glad when He reveals where they might not be healthy. We should gladly cooperate with Him and make any necessary changes. If we are bothered by correction we might be forsaking His way without even realizing it. Correction is necessary to maintain heart health.

ಬ Merry ೞ

A merry heart makes a cheerful countenance: but by sorrow of the heart the spirit is broken. The heart of him that has understanding seeks knowledge: but the mouth of fools feeds on foolishness. All the days of the afflicted are evil: but he that is of a merry heart has a continual feast.

Proverbs 15:13-15

The Lord is addressing our inner man — our hearts. There will be times when our inner man is touched by the inevitable pain of tragedy. Our spirits go through times of heaviness and brokenness. This is healthy and a time to draw near to the God of all comfort. This is a time to seek knowledge and grow in understanding.

There truly is a time and season for every purpose under heaven. There is a time of famine and a time to cry. We grow through these times in empathy, compassion and the ability to give others the very comfort we have received. The Lord comforts those who mourn and will bring us back to a place where the joy of His salvation is restored. We will find our hearts merry again. Our countenances will be revived and we will once again taste and see that the Lord is good.

We must be careful when we have sorrow of heart. We must not feed on foolishness but cry out to the Lord for knowledge and understanding. We will come through these times and eventually feast continually. The joy of the Lord is our strength and the merriness of our hearts will return through His healing and comfort.

❧ Choose ☙

Better is little with the fear of the LORD than great treasure and trouble with it. Better is a dinner of herbs where love is, than a stalled ox and hatred with it.

Proverbs 15:16-17

Better is a little with the fear of the Lord. In our desires to accumulate more or better things, we might be tempted to do things in haste. We might not consult the Lord for His plan concerning such ventures. We should move carefully when considering a new source of income, putting something on credit or taking on side jobs. We can end up with a treasure of trouble. We should seek the Lord regarding financial decisions, moving with the fear of Him. This means that our own desires and plans are laid before His feet and we seek His final confirmation or denial of our pursuits.

Better is a dinner of herbs with love. If someone strives to produce the *perfect meal* out of pride they could end up snapping at their children or guests. The atmosphere changes for the worse and the food loses its appeal. Perhaps a simple dinner of grilled cheese and tomato soup with a happy cook served with love would be much more impressive than the homemade lasagna accompanied with complaints. Let us be people who move carefully in the accumulation of things and preparation of meals.

ᛒ Quarrels ᴄᴈ

A wrathful man stirs up conflict: but he that is slow to anger appeases conflict.

Proverbs 15:18

Conflict can show us whether we are easily angered. This often manifests itself as impatience, a critical spirit or a snappy tongue. This might be a sign to us that we stir up conflict. Compromise can create an inner conflict that manifests itself in our relationships. When we have clean consciences we get along with others much better. Dealing with sin in our lives will help us have mercy on others. Is there something the Lord has shown you to confess *and* forsake?

"He that covers his sins shall not prosper: but whoever confesses and forsakes them shall have mercy." (Proverbs 28:13)

⁎ Thorns Å

*The way of the lazy man is as a hedge of thorns: but
the way of the righteous is free from obstacles.*

Proverbs 15:19

When we handle our responsibilities in lazy ways
our paths will have many obstacles and become very
unpleasant. A hedge of thorns on our paths means
that we would have to keep track of every
movement so we won't be poked and hurt by these
bushes. When we are half-hearted at work or home,
our paths become filled with things we are trying to
avoid. We are not enjoying our journeys. Things that
we should have finished and finished thoroughly,
loom in our paths yelling at us that they are
incomplete or need more attention — like thorns
poking us along our ways.

The Lord equates diligence with righteousness. Did
you know hard work honors the Lord and diligence
is to be an attribute of those who follow Him? When
our hands find something to do, we should do it
with *all* our might. When we are asked to do
something we should do it heartily as to the Lord. A
life of ease and pleasure propagates a life of
depression and purposelessness. We will feel like we
are dead while we are living if we are people who sit
down to eat and drink and only rise up to play.
Believers, honor the Lord, remove the hedge, and
enjoy a clear path as you seek to avoid laziness for
His glory.

❧ Offspring ❧

A wise son makes a glad father: but a foolish man despises his mother.

Proverbs 15:20

When our children are foolish the *mother* seems to feel the brunt of it. When they are doing well the *father* seems so proud. Mothers need not question the weight they often feel when they see their children choose foolishly. Our children have free wills. This weight is appropriate and is to be a motivating force to come before the Lord and cast those burdens upon Him. He will sustain us. The weight of children living without the fear of the Lord, is intolerable for the human soul. We must take the time, if only for 5 minutes, throughout our days, to bow before the Lord in prayer and give this weight and our children to the Lord. May mothers refuse to carry this burden but rather bless their heavenly Father by casting it continually upon Him. We are the children of God. Let's live like wise sons today and make *our* heavenly Father glad.

ഇ Joy ര

*Foolishness is joy to him that is destitute of wisdom:
but a man of understanding walks uprightly.*

Proverbs 15:21

Finding ourselves enjoying foolish choices reveals a great lack of wisdom. Hasty decisions are often motivated by impulse and are usually not led by the Holy Spirit. Our spirits should fear going down the road of foolishness and should desire the peace of the road marked by wisdom. When we are people who want understanding we will walk uprightly.

Walking uprightly can be likened to an upright posture. When we are walking uprightly we can view everything around us. We are able to see the past, present and future. We are not stubborn, determined to go in a certain direction. We are looking for His leading whether it agrees with our desires or not. How long will we argue with love? The Lord loves us and desires to order our steps and show us His paths of life.

Lift up your eyes in those areas in which you are seeking His will. Be open to all of the angles and don't be afraid of His path. His paths are the paths of pleasantness. (Prov 3:17)

❧ Independence ☙

Without counsel purposes are disappointed: but in the multitude of counselors they are established.

Proverbs 15:22

Our society promotes and affirms independence. A self-made person who can think alone is extolled as virtuous and deemed successful. The Lord wants us to be people who are open to ideas, visions and strategies from Him, yet open to good hearty counsel from others. We can learn things by experience but we can learn things through other people's experiences as well.

Listening to others' counsel can be helpful in determining God's plans for our lives. The Lord will show us which counsel He wants to use to establish His purposes. We should genuinely listen to the advice of others, knowing God may be speaking to us through others' insight. When we do this we take a position of humility, and humility comes before honor. If we consistently act independently we may be arrogant and wise in our own eyes. Pride comes before destruction. He doesn't want us disappointed due to lack of counsel. The Holy Spirit flows in the midst of seekers clothed in humility. May our purposes be established in the multitude of counselors.

❧ Timing ☙

A man has joy by the answer of his mouth: and a word spoken in due season, how good it is!

Proverbs 15:23

The words we use impact the amount of joy we have. Sometimes we can answer things hastily, give information we shouldn't, be critical or answer in some way that would create tension and grief in our relationships. If our verbal responses are guided by the Lord, we will have joy. Fruit, eaten in the right season, tastes sweet and perfect. If it is eaten before it is ripe the texture is often tough and the taste is minimal. If the fruit is eaten after the season, it is usually mushy and sour. Our words should come at a timing the Lord directs. Our very dispositions can be greatly affected by the words and tone we use in relationships.

Be slow to speak today and sensitive to Your Heavenly Gardener and what He wants to harvest from your mouth.

ஒ Above ை

The way of life is above to the wise, so that he may depart from hell beneath.

Proverbs 15:24

When we set our minds on things above, we will walk on the paths of life. If we get entangled with this world and the lures it puts before us, it will be hell. The world lies under the influence of the evil one and we ought to be suspicious of its priorities and value system. We must look *up* for instructions, wisdom and judgment. We must spend time with the Lord in order to have a life that is free from unnecessary conflict and confusion. If we are to experience good paths, we are to be people who see our citizenship in heaven and our King as the Lord. We ask Him for His counsel. We ask Him for His love. We ask Him for His ways. If we ask, we will receive. He lays up sound wisdom for the upright and is glorified in lives that are submitted to Him and His ways.

Don't expect natural responses to lead you into His ways. Expect the way above to guide you beyond the snares and lead you in the way everlasting.

ဿ Humility ☯

The LORD will destroy the house of the proud: but he will establish the border of the widow.

Proverbs 15:25

Pride is a dangerous thing. It is attributed to Lucifer and his rebellion against the Lord. It is connected to destruction. It is blamed for stubbornness and is one of the things the Lord hates.

If we are determined to control our homes, work places or lives, we are causing destruction. The proud person knows nothing and his personality is grating. The proud person is wise in their own opinion and gets frustrated when others conduct their lives in ways that contradict their expectations.

A widow in bible days was vulnerable and knew she lacked resources to survive. She was dependent on others to help her. She was humble and not self-confident. God will establish those who know they need His help and show the proud they aren't as great as they think they are.

ও Thoughts ব

The thoughts of the wicked are an abomination to the LORD: but the words of the pure are pleasant words.

Proverbs 15:26

The thoughts of the wicked are an abomination to the Lord. An "abomination" is something that is absolutely repulsive and offensive. Wicked people think up wicked things. These thoughts are sometimes developed into screenplays, song lyrics, scripts and advertisements. Pornographic photo shoots are thought out by the wicked. Burglaries and murders are thought out by the wicked. These are an abomination to the Lord. Discretion is needed when choosing input. We must guard our minds. Consider the input in our lives. Do we have the thoughts of the wicked influencing our perspectives or the words of the pure?

ও Greed ଓ

He that is greedy of gain troubles his own house; but he that hates bribes shall live.

Proverbs 15:27

There is nothing wrong with taking advantage of financial opportunities, but when there is an *I-want-more* attitude rooted in a lack of contentment, we will trouble our own households.

Greed tells us we need "a little more". Discontentment creates an agitated spirit. We might pursue gain without noticing what we might lose in the process.

Gain is not bad. Being greedy for gain *is*. Greed creates passion that overrides a submission to the priorities God has for us. Greed blinds us to true riches. Greed creates trouble along with the gain.

Let's be sure that when we pursue gain, we are maintaining gratefulness and contentment for what we currently have. This will protect our lives from the trouble greed promises to bring.

ೞ Studying ೕ

The heart of the righteous studies to answer: but the mouth of the wicked pours out evil things.

Proverbs 15:28

As people of God we must be people who do not answer a matter quickly. We study to answer. Studying involves looking at something with the intent of getting the right answer when tested. Part of our ability to speak the right things is, *"Are we studying the right things?"* Our hearts should be pondering the truths of God's Word in order to have His wisdom and grace upon our lips. Often our feelings, opinions and analysis shouldn't be shared. We can discuss our opinions with the Lord, but to give an answer we should take the time to give the *right* answer — the answer HE desires us to give. In order to be wise people, our words should be dedicated to His glory and purposes. Words are very powerful and we want the right power to come forth.

Commit your words to the Lord today. Be slow to speak and study to give the right responses.

❧ Disregard ☙

*The LORD is far from the wicked: but he hears the
prayer of the righteous.*

Proverbs 15:29

Direct rebellion against God's Word demonstrates a
lack of desire and submission to God's voice and
person. A wicked person is deciding that
communication with God is *not* wanted and
fellowship with God is *not* important.

If we desire a relationship with sin more than a
relationship with God, we will sense that God is far
from us. He will seem like a distant observer as
opposed to being actively involved in our lives. If we
are in wickedness and we sense that God is far, our
choices have spoken to Him that we don't want Him
near. We must forsake wickedness and ask for
forgiveness and fellowship. We must draw near to
Him and He will draw near to us. The blood of
Christ will wash our sins away, declare us righteous,
our prayers will be heard, and His presence will be
near.

‽ Stability ⧆

The light of the eyes rejoices the heart: and a good report makes strong bones.

Proverbs 15:30

What we listen to affects our inner man. Our hearts are the seats of our affections and emotions. Our bones represent our frames and ability to stand and weather life's challenges. A good perspective will fight depression and troubled hearts. What are we looking at? What articles are we reading? What shows are we watching? How are we looking at others? Images our minds think on come through our eyes. May this be our resolve: *I will set no evil thing before my eyes. I will choose to look at people and situations through the eyes of Your Word and counsel.*

When we listen to bad reports, our frames can start to weaken causing instability. When we hear good reports, we enjoy our relationships and desire to invest in people. Let's use caution in what we say and hear about others. We must strengthen our inner man to be upright and stable.

⁖ Correctable ⁍

The ear that hears the correction of life abides among the wise. He that refuses instruction despises his own soul: but he that hears correction gets understanding.

Proverbs 15:31-32

As followers of Christ, we have made ourselves correctable. When we realized that we have sinned and fallen short of the glory of God, we acknowledged that truly we have done wrong. If we are people who know we have done wrong, we should remain in a place of correction.

The people the Lord puts around us may have insight into us that we cannot see. By listening to correction and instruction, we will be wise people building our homes up to code. A humble mind will bow before correction, asking the Lord if it is true and how to respond.

"Correction" is pointing out what is wrong and "instruction" is showing how to get it right. These are two forms that should be the *Siamese twins* of parenting. When parents tell their children what they have done wrong, they should instruct them in the right way. This is how our Heavenly Father parents us. We must be examples of people who hear correction and do not refuse instruction.

❧ Honor ☙

The fear of the LORD is the instruction of wisdom;
and before honor is humility.

Proverbs 15:33

True humility only comes from the fear of the Lord. The fear of the Lord is clean and allows us to focus on *one* authoritative voice. This allows us to hear the voice of God above all other voices.

We need to be in a place where obedience to Him is all we are seeking in any given situation. We are to be more concerned with His leading than anyone else's response or reaction to our decisions. Clear instruction comes when we desire to please Him above everyone else involved. We must be willing to be ridiculed or judged in order to follow through with the Lord's leading. This is humility and it will result in honor.

If we are consciously more concerned with God's mind and heart than anyone else's, including our own, we will most certainly be in a receptive place. We will be able to distinguish God's wisdom. We will be ready to follow His voice as He speaks to us in the midst of confusing and complex situations.

ℬ Ideas ℭ

The preparations of the heart in man, and the answer of the tongue, is from the Lord.

Proverbs 16:1

As believers, our hearts are under the influence of the Lord. The Lord puts thoughts in our minds as we are thinking. The Lord, Himself, is breathing His purposes into us. We shouldn't be quick to dismiss the ideas that arise within us without asking the Lord if He is speaking.

We should be sensitive to His still, small voice when considering getting involved in something. Our answers are not to be based on our own desires or limitations alone. The answers we are supposed to give are from the Lord. Let's be slow to speak and consider whether the Lord is moving upon our hearts.

What have we been receiving from the Lord lately? How might the things we have been learning be related to a current discussion or opportunity? The Lord often prepares our hearts before we must give an answer. Let's be aware that our answers will direct our courses and we know His course for us is the one we should be walking on.

❧ Intents ❧

All the ways of a man are clean in his own eyes; but the Lord weighs the spirits.

Proverbs 16:2

We tend to think we are right when we evaluate our actions and deeds based upon our *own* criteria. The Lord weighs our spirits. He checks our hearts and deep-rooted motivations. When we are seeking to please the Lord, we should ask Him to help us be open to His evaluation of our spirits.

Instead of always bringing our actions before Him, let us approach Him with a desire to be searched and diagnosed deep within our frames. He is able to find and correct things we might never have known existed. His Word is like a surgeon's tool and is able to divide the thoughts and intents of our hearts. We may consider something worthless when He says it is valuable. We may consider something weighty when He judges it to be frivolous. He weighs our spirits and helps balance us out.

Let's not trust our own scales but be open and vulnerable to being weighed by the One who judges righteously.

ಕಿ Works ಚಿ

Commit your works to the Lord, and your thoughts shall be established.

Proverbs 16:3

Our society emphasizes the proper mindset in order to be successful in our pursuits. The Lord is telling us just the opposite. He is instructing us to commit our works, *all* we *do*, to Him and *then* our thoughts will be established. We will think the way He wants us to think.

As we go throughout our days; grocery shopping, running errands, cooking dinner, preparing reports, carrying out our job responsibilities, let us consciously commit these works to Him for His glory. Watch our thinking become settled and established, *not* chaotic and restless.

❧ Creator ☙

The Lord has made all things for himself: yes, even the wicked for the day of evil.

Proverbs 16:4

It is a sobering fact to consider we are products of a Creator and His plans and purposes.

We are the created ones and it is very much our responsibility to humble ourselves before Him and seek *His* purposes for our existence. All we see and all we own is here for *Him*. Until we realize this, we will experience seemingly empty and unfulfilled lives.

When we trust the wicked things that have happened to us are intended to accomplish His purposes, we will no longer feel like victims. We will be able to face our lives with hope and life. If our plans have excluded this important perspective, it would be wise to bring our stories before a faithful and powerful Creator. We should declare that even the wicked things that have happened to us are used by Him to bring about the quality of life He has created us to experience.

ஐ Majority ௸

Every one that is proud in heart is an abomination to the Lord: though hand join in hand, he shall not be unpunished.

Proverbs 16:5

The majority does *not* determine righteousness. Sometimes the most charismatic and influential people can steer opinion in a direction that is contrary to the Lord. With the humble there is wisdom and an ability to choose what is right apart from others agreeing with us.

When we are making arrogant decisions we might feel compelled to seek affirmation from others. Our decisions should be rooted in pleasing the Lord alone. When we are satisfied with pleasing the Lord, we will not need the approval of others. When we are doing what is right in the eyes of the Lord, we can stand alone.

❧ Iniquity ☙

By mercy and truth iniquity is purged; and by the fear of the Lord men depart from evil.

Proverbs 16:6

There are two things we need to do when confronting sin in ourselves and others. These two responses must be put together to purge sin. These two ingredients are *mercy* and *truth*.

Mercy involves not dealing out judgment with penalties. "Mercy" is being able to see how harshly something should be dealt with, but choosing to give less than what is deserved. It is an attitude of forgiveness.

"Truth" is looking at something for what it is according to God's judgment. If we want to deal with sin we have to see it for what God says it is. No excuses. No compromise. Call it what it is.

We are not to act like a sin isn't committed against us. This would be ignoring truth. If we recognize the sin with a high-minded approach, we ignore mercy. If we see a sin within us and respond with defeat, we ignore mercy. If we consider ourselves free from conviction, we ignore truth.

It is by mercy *and* truth that sin will no longer have the dominion and effect it wants to have within us and our relationships. The Lord has dealt with sin with mercy and truth and we would be wise to follow His example.

May we embrace the truth of conviction, extending and receiving mercy.

ಒ Enemies ೧

*When a man's ways please the Lord, he makes even
his enemies to be at peace with him.*

Proverbs 16:7

When we experience conflict we must choose how
to respond. We should turn our eyes upward and
seek how *God* would want us to respond.

Conflict wants to entangle and distract us from what
the Lord is calling us to do. We must not allow
conflict to disrupt our spiritual disciplines. When we
experience conflict in relationships, we must all the
more, position ourselves to hear from God and do
what pleases Him.

This means not only pleasing Him in the conflict,
but also in all areas of our lives. When we face
turbulent times we can start going astray without
even being aware of it. Conflict seeks to demand
our full attention. We must intentionally position
ourselves to hear from God. We must not allow
conflict to bully us into hasty decisions or
destructive responses.

We are not promised we won't have enemies. But
when our ways please the Lord, we will at least have
peace with them.

❧ Little ☙

Better is a little with righteousness than great revenues without it.

Proverbs 16:8

Our ability to esteem what is better is often tainted by imperfect judgment. The Lord wants us to know what is better. We must reject treasures gained by deception or wicked schemes. It is better to end up with less in our pockets and more treasures in heaven.

We must choose to do what is right even if it results in loss of material gain. We must believe that it is *better* to do right even if it is at the expense of profit. A guilty conscience competes with any enjoyment from ill-gotten riches. If we have to use unrighteousness to get something it is not the Lord's will for us to have it. The joy of the gift will not be there. If we have done this, we should seek to restore the gain and free ourselves from this wrongdoing.

He has a *better* life for us. Let's live this *better* life and define the quality of our lives by His scales.

๑ Directed ๛

A man's heart devises his way: but the Lord directs his steps.

Proverbs 16:9

Oftentimes we have ideas and plans. We bring these before the Lord and seek Him to direct our steps. The steps are the outward manifestation of the inward ideas.

In order to reach a destination we have to travel. The Lord wants to direct each step of the ideas that come into our hearts. We should acknowledge Him in all of our ways and be sensitive to the leading of His Holy Spirit. He will tell us what to do first, what is not important and what is to be a priority.

Just as He led His people through the wilderness, the Lord continues to be the One who can lead us through each of our days. We must not be stubborn, but flexible and yielding to His leading. He knows of obstacles and opportunities we might be blind to.

Oh Lord, lead us in Your ways. Show us how to carry out the ideas and plans You put in our hearts.

ಌ Directions ೞ

A divine sentence is in the lips of the king: his mouth is not to make mistakes in judgment.

Proverbs 16:10

The authority God has put over us is divine. He has set people over us to guide us in *His* ways. If we would *naturally* go in a certain direction then we wouldn't need people outside of us implementing boundaries. If our managers ask us to do something then we most likely wouldn't have chosen that task ourselves. Our husbands, parents or those in leadership often make decisions we most likely weren't going to choose for ourselves.

This means that the divine sentencing in our lives is often given through people God has set over us. We must consider the decisions of those in authority when they do not conflict with God's Word, as divine sentences. We can approach these decisions with gratefulness and consider the fact that the Lord might very well be using them to protect, challenge and direct us in ways we might never have chosen ourselves.

೫ Weighing ೬

An accurate weight and balance are the Lord's: all the weights of the bag are his work.

Proverbs 16:11

Proper evaluation requires good judgment. In bible times scales were instruments that had a weight on one side and a small plate on the other. They would put items such as stones in a bag on one side and the items being purchased on the other. It was called a balance. When the two were even with each other, a consumer was confident his purchase was weighed accurately.

There were swindlers in those days that would remove some stones from the bag and deceive the buyer into paying for more than they were receiving. They were weighing things inaccurately. When we are weighing things in our own lives we must remember the weights of the bag are His work.

We are capable of weighing things inaccurately. We can undervalue something that deserves great esteem and consider something weighty that is to be disregarded. God's scale uses the weight of His Word. Staying in His Word will help us determine the weights of all we face and encounter.

ᛒᚩ Authority ᚳᚱ

It is an abomination for kings to commit wickedness:
for the throne is established by righteousness.
Righteous lips are the delight of kings; and they love
him that speaks right. The wrath of a king is as
messengers of death: but a wise man will pacify it. In
the light of the king's countenance is life; and his
favor is as a cloud of the latter rain.

Proverbs 16:12-15

People in authority are responsible to exercise
authority in righteousness. Position is not given in
order to give the person advantage. Leadership is
established to implement what is right. A leader is
to make decisions that are righteous. They are to be
impartial and concerned for the well-being of those
they lead.

Leaders will make better decisions when they have
the right people around them. They should
surround themselves with people who have a
genuine interest in benefiting the organization.
People who are slow to speak, able to forecast
problems as well as offer practical solutions,
contribute to a leader's success.

If someone in authority is angry, wisdom is able to
calm them down. A wise person will seek to find out
the reason for the anger and work towards turning
things around or giving comfort. When a leader
looks favorably on someone, it makes that person's
life much smoother. Pacifying anger, speaking good
things and caring for the leader, all contribute to
successful leadership and a pleasant environment
for all those under his authority.

ଓ Money ଔ

How much better is it to get wisdom than gold! And to get understanding rather than silver!

Proverbs 16:16

It is tempting to place money on the throne of our lives. We may agree to certain commitments *just* because we are getting paid for them. Making commitments solely upon financial gain can rob us of other opportunities. We may miss out on more valuable times such as bible study, family time or ministry.

The wisdom the Lord wants to give us is *much* more valuable than gold. Understanding is to be chosen *rather* than silver. This means money *alone* should never determine our commitments or priorities. Wisdom will evaluate the worthiness of a pursuit. When we obey wisdom, we prosper.

Seek not to be rich. Seek to listen and obey Him.

❧ Roads ☙

The highway of the upright is to depart from evil: he that keeps his way protects his soul.

Proverbs 16:17

The highway of the upright is to depart from evil. When we are tempted or are exposed to that which God considers evil, we must determine our road. Our highways are to be paved with choices that depart from evil. We don't need to analyze the evil, consider it, explore it or understand it. Rather, we must *depart* from it. Turn off that television. Shut off the computer. Walk away from that person. Drive past that place. Get in the car and go. Walk out of the room.

We will preserve our souls. Our souls include our emotions and intellect. When we watch where we are going, we will not have to deal with unnecessary decay and corruption to our hearts and minds.

May we realize that many times the Lord truly does deliver us *from* evil. Other times *we* must make the choice and *depart* from it.

Lord, use Your word today to light our highways and may Your Holy Spirit show us how to guard our ways and *depart* from evil.

ೞ Lowly ೞ

Pride goes before destruction, and an arrogant spirit before a fall. Better it is to be of a humble spirit with the lowly, than to divide the spoil with the proud.

Proverbs 16:18-19

Humility is something *we* are responsible for. We are told over and over again to humble *ourselves*. Like a helium balloon, our old nature keeps rising up, demanding we think more highly of ourselves than we should. It is better to be of a humble spirit. It is better to be with humble people than those who praise themselves.

The Lord keeps telling us in this book of wisdom what is better. We would be wise to believe Him. When we are stubborn, we are setting ourselves up for destruction. If we are already on our faces, we cannot fall. If we are on our faces, He can lift us up. Let's humble ourselves under the mighty hand of God in order to have Him exalt us in due season.

&) Trusting (&

He that handles a matter wisely shall find good: and whoever trusts in the Lord, happy is he. The wise in heart shall be called prudent: and the sweetness of the lips increases learning. Understanding is a wellspring of life to him that has it: but the instruction of fools is foolishness. The heart of the wise teaches his mouth, and adds learning to his lips.

Proverbs 16:20-23

Handling situations with wisdom assures us good things will come. Choosing to make wise decisions even if they are difficult, demonstrates that we trust God. We come to a place where His wisdom is valued and treasured. We no longer have to analyze and concoct plans based on random ideas to handle our lives. We seek Him and He assures us His ways are right. Happiness follows and our lives flow. We experience His plans and discover they are best. Our lips will give good answers and we will learn from making right decisions. Our hearts will treasure what God says is valuable and we will be empowered to continue speaking what is right.

God wants His people skilled in life. When our lives are defined by His counsel we demonstrate what it is like to be under the reliable counsel of our God.

❧ Honeycomb ☙

Pleasant words are like honeycomb, sweet to the soul, and health to the bones.

Proverbs 16:24

Words are very powerful. A word spoken at the right time has the potential to sweeten even the most bitter life.

Honeycomb was considered a treat and brought much needed strength to those travelling through barren regions with minimal supplies. When the traveler would find the honeycomb and take in the sweet substance, their strength would be restored. The dreary, dusty path became more pleasant. When we speak pleasant words, we can have this effect on those traveling around us.

When we wake up our children in the morning, we can speak pleasant words. When our husbands come home from work, we can speak pleasant words. When our wives seem weary and depleted from their days, we can speak pleasant words. When we answer our phones, our tone can be pleasant and sweet. When we come before that cashier we can speak words that will be sweet to their soul and health to their bones.

May the Lord touch our tongues today and may the words we speak be pleasant and sweet, bringing health to those around us.

℘ Perspectives ℘

There is a way that seems right to a man, but the end are the ways of death.

Proverbs 16:25

It is important for us to know the criteria we use to make decisions. Our decisions can seem right but the end of those choices could be death. This is where the Word of God and good, godly counsel comes in. We should not trust *ourselves*. Seeking God's affirmation or redirection through His Word is imperative. Running our decisions by a person who loves the Lord and loves us could help us avoid tragic results. Certain rivers look calm and beautiful but there might be a deadly drop downstream. A quaint road might have a bridge out ahead. God is the one who was, is and is to come. We must not trust our own understanding. It is always healthy to remain open to God's redirects and resist any stubbornness we might have. What may seem right to us, may not be the best decision. We must remain humble, open to correction and willing to change our minds.

❧ Cravings ☙

He that labors, labors for himself; for his mouth
craves it of him.

Proverbs 16:26

When someone is hungry they are motivated *to do*
what it takes to satisfy that hunger. If someone
knows they need to make money to buy food, they
can perform their tasks diligently with a sense of
ownership. They want to keep their job because they
know their daily bread is coming from that source.

If we don't *hunger* for righteousness, we might not
be *laboring* for righteousness. When we are doing
what He has called us to do, we develop a godly
hunger. We crave His will because we have tasted
how good it is. In order to maintain stamina to
continue in these works, we hunger for more of Him
and His strength. If we have not been hungering for
God, there are two things we can do. Stop and ask
Him for this hunger and evaluate our level of
activity in His kingdom's business. Let's examine our
hunger for His kingdom by evaluating our daily
activities. Is God's kingdom seen in the list of things
we plan to do? Is there a lack of attention and
involvement in His kingdom? This could be
contributing to a lack of hunger for the things of
God because we are not burning spiritual *calories?*
Let's be open to see if our lack of hunger may very
well be due to a lack of kingdom activity.

❧ Information ☙

An ungodly man digs up evil: and in his lips there is as a burning fire. A twisted man sows conflict: and a whisperer separates close friends.

Proverbs 16:27-28

Sometimes we can get information that is not meant to be repeated. Information that makes its way to our ears is not necessarily to be delivered to those who are affected by or involved with it. Before we repeat something we should stop and ask the Lord if this information could be a juicy morsel the adversary wants to use to separate the closest of friends. Information is not always given to us in order to inform others. Information could be given that we might pray over a situation or learn from it. We shouldn't dig up evil. We do not need to inquire into matters the Lord has not asked us to search out. We shouldn't use information given in confidence to sow seeds of division or discouragement.

ஐ Enticed ௸

A violent man entices his neighbor, and leads him into the way that is not good. He shuts his eyes to devise twisted things: moving his lips he brings evil to pass.

Proverbs 16:29-30

Whom we choose to spend time with is very important. We shouldn't follow those who lead us into the way that is not good. They like to entice people to go in directions that are not good. We should seek better company. A group mentality usually accompanies evil choices. Perhaps having someone along helps these types of people justify their actions and share the blame.

Stay sober and alert. The enemy is seeking to devour and will use people around you. Ask the Lord to search your friendships and bring those who call upon Him out of pure heart into your life. Don't feel you owe anyone your submission. Submit to God and follow Him!

৪৩ Age ৪৩

A gray-haired head is a crown of glory, if it be found in the way of righteousness.

Proverbs 16:31

Age is a crown of glory. There is a condition though. This age must be accompanied with the way of righteousness. If someone lives a long life in rebellion to God and in the bitterness of their own thinking, the gray head is *not* a crown of glory.

When we meet an elderly brother or sister in Christ who is living for the Lord, we had best stop and listen. They have a perspective we do not have and their counsel and observations are highly valuable. They have seen the faithfulness of God and know the brevity of life. They know they are close to seeing the Lord face-to-face and their insight is rooted in eternity.

Lord, bring us those saints who will give us perspective and wisdom rooted in age accompanied with righteousness.

๒ Reactions ૪

He that is slow to anger is better than the mighty;
and he that rules his spirit than he that takes a city.

Proverbs 16:32

Our culture esteems loud and pushy people as mighty and often influential. Those who submit their anger to Him will be called mighty. The one who can rule their own spirit will accomplish great victories.

When we are around our children, spouses or co-workers different triggers may provoke us. These are the times we must call upon the Lord asking Him to rule over us. Then we can rule over our own spirits and reactions. We are never forced to blow up or give in to wrath.

When Jesus came into the temple and knocked over the tables, he did something interesting first. John 2:14-15 tells us: *"And found in the temple those that sold oxen and sheep and doves, and the changers of money sitting: And when he had made a whip of small cords, he drove them all out of the temple..."* When he found these people wrongfully selling in the temple, he did not react suddenly. He made a whip of small cords. He got the materials together. He focused on making it. He was in control.

When we are provoked, perhaps justifiably, we should rule over our spirits and not react in haste. Consider what sort of reaction should be woven together. Let our responses be designed by the Lord so the reactions are from Him and please Him.

❧ Chance ❧

The lot is cast into the lap; but the whole disposing of it is of the Lord.

Proverbs 16:33

Some things seem to happen by chance but truly the Lord is in these events as well. Our days can take directions that seem haphazard and non-directed but the whole disposing is of the Lord. When we commit our days to Him, we can sit back and enjoy watching His sovereign hand in all that comes our way. We are not victims. We are His vessels and He places us in situations and environments with purpose in mind. As you go throughout this day, remember nothing is by chances to the child of God. Trust that your day is under His Sovereign hand.

ಸ Quietness ೡ

Better is a dry morsel, and quietness with it, than a house full of sacrifices with conflict.

Proverbs 17:1

This particular proverb is contrasting two meals. One is a meal that consists of a dry piece of bread and the other has a variety of wonderfully cooked meats. There is peace at the first meal and the other has frustration, complaining and contention. God tells us the first one is better.

If preparing a *wonderful* meal makes you a major pain in the *you-know-what*, it is *not* worth it. If what you are cooking puts you in high-stress mode you might need to downsize and reduce your expectations.

Better are grilled cheese sandwiches with a happy mom or dad than barbecued ribs and a frustrated cook. Better is frozen chicken nuggets and canned green beans with love and tenderness than an extravagant meal and contention. Better are quesadillas on paper towels with joy than homemade enchiladas with an angry wife. Better is a bowl of cereal with peace than marinated top sirloin with a resentful papa. When planning your meals, still your heart and prepare it before you prepare the meal.

ಐ Promotion ೞ

A wise servant shall have rule over a son that causes shame, and shall have part of the inheritance among the brethren.

Proverbs 17:2

People are promoted because of what they *do*, not what *position* they currently *hold*. Promotion will be given to those who can carry out the task best. Opportunities open up for people who walk in wisdom and don't cause problems.

In our homes, workplaces or ministries we should make it a goal to walk in wisdom and bring honor to those who rule over us. When we do this, we are a blessing to those we serve. When our names comes up, faithfulness and diligence will be associated with them.

Ꮽ Hearts Ꮳ

The fining pot is for silver, and the furnace for gold:
but the Lord tries the hearts.

Proverbs 17:3

A fining pot is heated up to purify metals. The
elements that are impure come to the top and are
able to be removed by the goldsmith. The Lord is
likened to the fining pot. He is the One who can
have the same effect on our hearts. Our hearts can
have hidden hurts, bitterness, pride or confusion.
The Lord wants our hearts cleansed of these things.
When we spend time in His presence and pour out
our hearts before Him, His holy fire will search us.
That which should be confessed and forsaken often
comes to the surface. There is no fear in love and the
fire of His presence is never to be feared. Anything
He wishes to reveal in us is intended for our good
and His glory. As we grow in the knowledge of Him,
we will clearly see what needs to be removed. We
may think the Lord is dealing with our behavior,
when it is the heart behind it He wishes to purify.

ℬ Lies ℭ

A wicked doer gives heed to false lips; and a liar gives ear to a spiteful tongue.

Proverbs 17:4

When we are consistently doing what the Lord doesn't want us to do, we are giving heed to false lips. There is some sort of lie that we believe *every* time we choose to obey temptation or go beyond the boundaries the Lord has for us. It would be good to ask the Lord to reveal the lies we believe in our hearts that are empowering us to go in the way of wickedness.

Lies accompany temptation. When we are tempted we should listen for lies. Then, with the help of the Holy Spirit, we should speak the truth and obey. The devil is the father of all lies and it is with a lie he brought down Eve. We, as believers, should learn from her and remember that if lies worked to cause humans to err in the past, lies can work in the future. We should rather hear the truth and obey it!

‽ Calamities ∞

Whoever mocks the poor reproaches his Maker: and he that is glad at calamities shall not be unpunished.

Proverbs 17:5

We can grow weary of the demands around us. There will always be people in need. The poor we will always have with us. We must never be glad at the calamities in a poor person's life even if it is their own fault. The Lord takes this very seriously. Many times due to an addiction or laziness, people may find themselves in need. It is not our place to mock them. We should be willing to point them to their Maker who is able to rescue them from such patterns. Others find themselves in need due to health issues or even being a victim of someone's selfish gain.

When we meet people in need let us be cautious in our responses. Let's be sympathetic to their plight regardless of the cause and ask the Lord what our response should be. Let's never be high minded but humble and know their Maker is watching out for them.

ℬ Generations ℭ

Children's children are the crown of old men; and the
glory of children are their fathers.

Proverbs 17:6

Grandchildren are to be treasured by grandfathers.
When a man's children have children he can see
what has been passed on to the next generation. A
man must remember his influence on his own
children is intended to continue to the following
generation. These grandchildren are direct
descendants of their parents' fathers. A man must
take his position as a father seriously, knowing
children that have yet to be born will be affected by
the childhood their parents had.

Secondly, a father who walks in integrity brings a
quality of life to their children. Fathers are meant to
be highly esteemed by their children. It is important
for mothers to point out admirable qualities they see
in their children's fathers. This will help their
children have a more glorious childhood.

If we don't have any children, we can certainly
influence other children to see their fathers in the
light of praise. We can ask children what they
admire about their fathers. We can be a part of
building up a Christian home, so when the enemy
comes in we will be part of the standard that the
Lord is raising up.

ॐ Words ॐ

Excellent speech is not becoming to a fool: much less do lying lips to a prince.

Proverbs 17:7

Our words often reveal who we are. Just as much as a foolish person speaking words of wisdom would catch us off guard, so too, lying lips don't fit a prince.

A prince has authority and is esteemed as one who is concerned for his father's kingdom. We are to be those princes wanting our heavenly Father's kingdom to be furthered and to rule in people's lives.

Lies are not becoming. We must care about representing situations in an accurate way. This requires having the fear of the Lord and being slow to speak. We can always answer *"I am not sure"*, when we are in doubt. We can answer *"I don't feel comfortable answering that question"*, when we don't want to give information. Truthful lips are controlled by the *Spirit of Truth* and show forth a life that desires to walk in truth.

Be careful about how you answer people. You must speak truth, not exaggerations or misrepresentations.

Proverbs 12:22 says, *"Lying lips are an abomination to the LORD: but they that deal truly are his delight."*

❧ Gifts ☙

A gift is as a precious stone in the eyes of him that has it: wherever it turns, it prospers.

Proverbs 17:8

Whatever we have received from the Lord is to be valued and seen as given to us for *HIS* purposes. All we have, has been *given* to us. We should seriously consider His purposes for these resources.

Our possessions, spiritual gifts, marriages, mates, jobs, children, money, and time; these are a few of the things that are meant to prosper. They are to be yielded to Him and used for His glory. Depression can set in when we are living and using what He has given us for ourselves, and *not* for Him. We can feel empty and unsuccessful.

Take a moment and commit all you have to Him. Ask Him to use the gifts He has given you in the way He desires to. Watch your days be filled with a strong sense of purpose and direction.

೫ Cover ೫

He that covers a transgression seeks love; but he that repeats a matter separates very friends.

Proverbs 17:9

Sometimes when we are sinned against we want to pull others into our pain. We are to *cover* a transgression if we are to seek *love*. When someone sins against us we should commit it to the Lord and seek Him for His heart of grace and forgiveness. We must be careful about who we repeat it to even *after* the offense has been forgiven.

Telling others about a sin can separate close friends. We often leave out details or present the situation in a way that elicits shock or anger. We can leave them in a place where they have to work through it. In the multitude of words, sin is not lacking.

When we talk to a friend recounting a story involving sin, we should not bring attention to the sin. We can share a general account that an offense was made and the Lord healed the relationship without repeating the details. We don't need to give a play-by-play account of what our adversary has done. He doesn't deserve air time. We should rather repeat, detail by detail all that the Lord has done and magnify Him.

If we need godly counsel, we should seek to recount the matter to one who is in spiritual authority. We could also speak with someone who doesn't know the offender. By bringing it to the light in the appropriate environment we seek love. When we forgive we can choose to not bring things to remembrance. This will make us like God who remembers our sins no more.

❧ Consequences ☙

*Correction enters more into a wise man than a
hundred stripes into a fool.*

Proverbs 17:10

The Lord wants us to be corrected by words more
than consequences. When confronted on actions or
attitudes, are we defensive or stubborn? If we don't
receive verbal correction, we might find ourselves
facing *a hundred stripes* instead. We should let the
Word of God or the correction of a godly friend do a
work in us. We can avoid needless wounds and
repercussions of foolish choices. We should embrace
God's standards and continually be open to His
correction and challenges. We should cooperate
with the deep work of correction producing lasting
transformation.

When was the last time you heard the voice of
correction? Has it entered your soul? Has it become
a part of your character and produced boundaries
you embrace? Give correction access to every area of
your being and watch God perfect your identity.

ℬ Rebellion ℭ

*An evil man seeks only rebellion: therefore a cruel
messenger shall be sent against him.*

Proverbs 17:11

Avoiding boundaries and authority is likened to evil.
There is often a demonic element within rebellion.
Rebellion is associated with being stubborn and self-
willed. When we choose our own will rather than an
appropriate leading of authority, we invite conflict
into our lives. The spirit of rebellion is rooted in
pride.

When we are pleasing the Lord we don't demand
our own way. It pleases the Lord when we seek to
come under authority in our lives in order to honor
Him.

If we don't, we will be hearing *cruel*
messengers....late fees, fines, parking tickets, court
hearings, etc. Let's submit to authority whenever it
does not contradict God's authority and enjoy the
fact that we will not be confronted by such cruel
messengers.

❧ Foolishness ☙

Let a bear robbed of her cubs meet a man, rather than a fool — his foolishness.

Proverbs 17:12

Bears are usually shy and easily frightened of humans. They will, however, defend their cubs. A ferocious, unrestrained reaction will proceed from a mama bear when her cubs are in danger.

The Lord is equating this violent rage in a bear to a person who is facing the obvious repercussions of foolish choices. They are unreasonable and ready to lash out at anyone within close proximity when faced with the consequences of their foolishness. A fool who is confronted with their foolishness is often easily-angered.

If you are facing consequences for a foolish choice, admit your foolishness, receive forgiveness and face the consequences, knowing God will help you through it.

ଈ Remember ଓ

Whoever rewards evil for good, evil shall not depart from his house.

Proverbs 17:13

When kindness is shown to us, it is wise to make a strong mental note of it. We must remember the kindness in the future. Sometimes the enemy can whisper suggestions of ill intent about someone who has done good to us. He will question their motives. He will offer suggestions of evil intentions in order to sow discord among the brethren. If we are not careful we might follow his suggestions and reward evil for good.

If we do this, our homes will be plagued with trouble. Consider who you might have gossiped about or been unkind to lately. Apart from this being wrong in and of itself, are the subjects of your actions people who have been kind to you? Be aware of your adversary's plot to have you reward evil for good.

How about your pastor or ministry leaders who are seeking to bless and equip you? Have you criticized and torn them down in the midst of their love and concern for your walk with the Lord? How about your husband who is seeking to take care of you and provide for you? How about your wife who often prepares such wonderful meals and keeps your house a home? How about your supervisor who has trained and equipped you?

May we take note of good shown to us and be guarded against rewarding evil for this good. This will protect our homes from unnecessary trouble and we will not cooperate with the accuser of the brethren.

୨୦ Contention ଓଃ

The beginning of conflict is as when one lets out water: therefore leave off contention, before it be meddled with.

Proverbs 17:14

Whenever an argument takes place, it has to start somewhere. The beginning of conflict is like letting a little water out of a dam. It trickles at first, but there is a great body of water behind it, ready to pour out on all that is in its path.

We must recognize when the water starts to trickle — when we are slightly annoyed or disagreeable. If we can picture a dam filled with the water of contention, we might be more guarded at the beginning of potential conflict.

The Lord tells us to leave this contentious state before it gets out of control. He is our rock and He is able to hold all of it back. Let's not be careless with our attitudes and responses. This will help us avoid releasing a flood of devastating words and actions.

ಶಂ Justify ಛ

*He that justifies the wicked, and he that condemns
the just, they are both an abomination to the Lord.*

Proverbs 17:15

The Lord hates when the wicked are justified.
Actions or motives that are evil according to the
Lord can be justified by human reason or thought.
The Lord hates this. It is an abomination. Whether it
is a psychologist's assessment, a supreme court's
ruling or a friend's hearty agreement, if *any*one is
justifying what God calls wicked, it is an
abomination. If it is a documentary on television, an
internet article or a scientific study, if they justify
sin, God hates this. If we, ourselves, justify what we
have done when, in fact, the Lord says it is wicked, it
is an abomination. We must be cautious when
giving reasons, that we do not justify wickedness nor
believe those who do.

The Lord hates it when the just are condemned. It is
an abomination to declare a righteous deed as
wrong when the Lord declares it to be righteous.
How often those who are doing His will are
condemned and judged evil by modern day
standards! How often those who are seeking to
please the Lord are labeled and declared extreme
and misfits of society! If we are labeled as such, we
should remember so were many of God's prophets.

The Lord is our judge. When He says something is
evil, it is evil. When the Lord says something is
right, it is right. Let us never justify the wicked or
condemn the just.

ঙ Pay ଓ

Why does a fool invest in trying to find wisdom,
seeing he has no heart to actually obey it?

Proverbs 17:16

To gain wisdom in our lives, there is a price to be paid. Wisdom is the higher road and takes focus *and* intent to stay on it. Voices within and voices without, will attempt to dissuade us from the wise way of living. We must ask the Lord for a heart that desires to choose the wise way in order to be willing to pay the price. Anything worth anything has a high price tag.

In order to enjoy lives that are ordered by wisdom, we must be people who are willing to pay the price of self-denial, self-control and waiting on the Lord. We will enjoy the benefits of a life that reflects the wisdom God has led us in. Our finances will be ordered, our eating habits will result in a good weight, our homes will be in order and our relationships will be free of foolish entanglements. There is a cost but the results are worth it!

&o Loyalty cs

A friend loves at all times, and a brother is born for adversity.

Proverbs 17:17

This world has cheapened the meaning of friendship. It is portrayed as mere companionship meant to enjoy the frivolities of life. Lighthearted relationships are defined by mutual interests or hobbies that provide social connections and laughter. The Lord has quite a different definition and function for friendships. If we are true friends, we step up conspicuously during times of adversity and make the burdens others are carrying, our concern. We should seek how we may help bear these burdens and desire to be vessels of the Lord's love and assistance in others' lives.

Friendship can be fun and lighthearted, but the true strength of the relationship is found in times of trouble. We need to love at *all* times. To be a good friend we should think of our friends as siblings. We have history and we anticipate a future with them. We trust that we have been placed into people's lives by a sovereign God who desires to use us to help and support them.

Our prayer lists should involve adversities that our friends are going through. We should seek to hear scripture or insight from the Lord to give them. Our worlds should not be self-defined, but include the burdens and seasons our friends are experiencing. When we do this we fulfill the law of Christ and have the same care one for another. This shows the world that we are His disciples by our love for one another.

᪄ Co-Signing ᪆

A man void of understanding strikes hands, and becomes a co-signer for a friend.

Proverbs 17:18

We may lack understanding if we become co-signers for friends. Our relationships may suffer as a result of this type of financial agreement. Dealing with money can change relationships. Co-signing on behalf of friends may require us to fulfill our friends' financial responsibilities if they fail to pay. When a friend does not meet a financial obligation we will be directly impacted by their irresponsibility. We might find ourselves bitter or resentful.

We can do this if we consider the loan our own and are willing to pay it out of love for our friends. We cannot come alongside a friend financially with contingencies and expectations without asking for a breeding ground of suspicion and bitterness. If we are unable to lend without expecting repayment, we should not lend. We should not be a co-signer. We should help with what we can give — no strings attached, and then put them in the Lord's hands for their financial dealings. We lack understanding by shaking hands on this sort of arrangement with a friend if we fail to assume the role as a giver rather than a co-signer.

When someone asks you to participate in any type of financial arrangement, seek the Lord. Do not say yes because it is your friend. You should pray even more about it because he or she is your friend. If you lack peace or consider yourself unable to pay the loan on your own without resentment if they fail, do not enter into such an agreement. Explain that you are not comfortable with this sort of arrangement and help them as the Lord leads. He loves them and He will take care of them. Perhaps their idea of a solution is not the Lord's.

৳ Transgression ଔ

He loves transgression that loves conflict: and he that exalts his gate seeks destruction.

Proverbs 17:19

Being attracted to sin and choosing to do it will lead to conflict in our lives. We will face conflict and tension associated with any sin that causes our lives to be weighed down unnecessarily. When we love a sin more than the Lord, we invite conflict into our lives.

As people who desire to have quiet spirits, hating sin is one way to nurture inner peace. Confronting the sin and asking the Lord to give us a hatred for it, will help us have the peace of God ruling in our hearts. This will deliver us from the tumultuous deception of sin.

Eve was deceived when she partook of the forbidden fruit and as a result we have conflict between our old sinful nature and that which is born of God. Choosing to obey the Lord in boundaries He has set, strengthens our new man which is created after Him in holiness and true righteousness. When we give in to sin, our old nature is fed and the conflict between the two grows fiercer.

Exalting our gates is a term used for self-confidence. In bible times there were gates to the cities that controlled what went in and what went out. A wall surrounded the city and these gates had to be strong enough to keep the enemy out when closed. If we are people who boast in our own abilities to resist sin and keep things out, we are exalting our gates. God says that if we do this, we seek destruction.

An arrogant spirit comes before destruction. It is important to strengthen our gates and seek the Lord for the right filters for our lives. It is quite a different thing than trusting in these precautions. Our dependency is to be in the Lord who is guarding our lives. Unless the Lord guards the house, we work hard with nothing to show for it. Unless the Lord is our watchman we will not have the resources to come against those unexpected attacks from the enemy of our souls. Let us boast in the Lord, seek to hate sin, and trust that He desires to protect us from conflict and destruction.

❧ Twisted ☙

He that has a twisted heart finds no good: and he that has a perverse tongue falls into mischief.

Proverbs 17:20

Brothers and sisters, what unnecessary conflict and burdens we end up carrying when our hearts and mouths are not subjected to the Lord! Let us find good today by asking the Lord to create in us clean hearts. Let's avoid falling into mischief by repeating matters accurately and giving information in the most truthful and loving way possible. Good things will come when we are quick to confess ugly thoughts and motives we may find within our hearts. Let's keep ourselves from falling by giving sound words rooted in God's truth and love. This makes days where we can anticipate finding good and avoid falling.

ℬ Training ℭ

He that gives birth and raises a fool does it to his sorrow: and the father of a fool has no joy.

Proverbs 17:21

Children are conceived in sin. There is a sinful, foolish nature we have all inherited. Parents are instructed to train children in the way they *should* go, not the way they *naturally* go. If parents ignore this great ministry and allow foolishness to reign and go undisciplined, they do it to their own sorrow and the father will not have joy.

Parents must not neglect or grow lazy in this commission. God defines what foolish behavior is. Parents can seek God as how to instruct and lead their children *away* from these things. Here are some examples of foolishness children must be trained away from:

- Not believing in the existence of God (Ps 14:1)
- Going after loose women, having sex outside of marriage (Prov 7:22)
- Hating someone but pretending to be nice to them with words (Prov 10:18)
- Speaking evil things about someone to paint them in a bad light (Prov 10:18)
- Doing mischievous things for fun or approval of others (Prov 10:23)
- Evaluating a course of action as right based on feelings apart from any sort of counsel or objective measurement (Prov 12:15)
- Self-confidence and boasting about being right in their own eyes (Prov 14:16)
- Being easily angered or annoyed by situations or people (Prov 14:17)

- Despising the advice of one's father (Prov 15:5)
- Trusting in one's own heart and feelings (Prov 28:26)
- Talking a lot without purpose and caution (Eccl 10:14)

Parents must be on the lookout for these foolish behaviors in their children. They must see to it that they pray, instruct, correct and exemplify the opposite of these types of behavior. If children take heed to this, parents can look forward to less sorrow and more joy.

❧ Medicine ☙

A merry heart does good like a medicine: but a broken spirit dries the bones.

Proverbs 17:22

When our hearts are merry, our bodies function better. When our inner man is troubled, our frames become brittle and unable to support us. A merry heart is not just an outward expression of joy but an inner state of mind. A merry heart is within us.

A merry heart knows it is accepted and loved by *no* merit of its own but by the finished work of the Lord Jesus Christ. A merry heart has a sense of purpose given by the One who dwells within it by faith. A merry heart is feasting on promises given by the One who never disappoints. A merry heart is considering all that the Lord has done for it. A merry heart is not weighed down with unconfessed sin. A merry heart is looking to be a source of blessing and refreshment to others. A merry heart recognizes the simplest events of the day as glimpses of God's faithfulness and love. A merry heart connects history with the present and anticipates the future being a further revelation of God's presence. A merry heart delights in a child's laughter, a dog's facial expression, a cake's decorated beauty, the smell of meat and onions being united in a hot pan, the clean, hot water of a morning shower, the soft, tender sheets that surround us as we sleep and other daily events that are often not appreciated or taken in.

By having the peace of God ruling in our hearts, we are free to absorb and enjoy a rich life. This does good, like medicine.

ເ Decisions ຕ

A wicked man bribes in secret in order to distort the ways of judgment.

Proverbs 17:23

Bribery is not good. It twists the mind of the one who has to make a clear call based upon what is good and right. Gifts, flattery and manipulation can contaminate righteous judgment. These can distort impartial evaluation and cloud good judgment.

When parenting children parents may melt with that four-year-old's sweet smile and not follow through with the appropriate consequence. A teenager can begin to bargain with his parents trying to change their minds regarding some sort of consequence already instated. A single believer might be tempted to lower their dating standards after receiving flattering words or a flirtatious look from an unbeliever. A wife may seek to persuade her husband to change his mind with sensuality or pouting. A husband may seek to influence his wife in an immoral direction by manipulating scripture or reason to get her to cooperate with him.

When we make judgments we must not allow influences to change our minds if those decisions are godly and good. If we don't like a decision someone makes that affects us, we should be cautious in trying to change their minds.

Our God is a Righteous Judge. Let's be sure that we respectfully submit to righteous judgments and not be people who allow flattery, favor or gifts to distort our judgment.

❧ Obvious ☙

*Wisdom is before him that has understanding; but
the eyes of a fool are in the ends of the earth.*

Proverbs 17:24

Wisdom is obvious to people who have
understanding. God's Word declares God's mind. If
we have been under the direct teaching of God's
Word we will understand what is valuable, what is
worthless, what is holy and what is sinful. As we
walk in a purposed reverence throughout our days
seeking to do things His way, wisdom will be right in
front of us.

Foolish people will be looking beyond their
immediate resources and responsibilities. They will
be looking for another mate, a different house, a
new job or some other source to provide an answer
and solution to their problems. Wandering eyes can
be a symptom of avoiding current situations.

We must look right before us and ask God to show
us solutions He has for our current situations. We
must guard our hearts from going to the *ends of the
earth* and rather look up to the God who promises to
put wisdom right in front of us.

Ask for understanding rather than hasty far-fetched
ideas that tempt you to look beyond the very life
God has asked you to live.

ಐ Fools ೞ

A foolish son is a grief to his father, and bitterness to her that gave birth to him.

Proverbs 17:25

When children do foolish things, parents' hearts are greatly affected. Parents can try to deny these feelings but bitterness and grief hit the hearts of mom and dad. This is why the ministry of parenting must not be trivialized. Parents are responsible to model and instruct their children in wisdom. Wisdom begins with the fear of the Lord.

If you are a parent, do your children see *you* making foolish and impulsive choices or do they see *you* waiting on the Lord and testing things against His Word? Do they see *you* and your mate praying together over decisions deciding to honor the Lord or do they see *you* both making decisions with your own understanding or reason?

The grief and bitterness that parents experience when and if their children choose to live foolishly, should never be rooted in the example that they set before them.

✌ Consider ✍

Also to punish the just is not good, nor to strike princes for equity.

Proverbs 17:26

I have on more than one occasion, dealt out a consequence only to find that the wrong child received the punishment. I was too quick and not calculated enough in discerning a matter.

When we punish the just, this is not good. Those in leadership should not punish someone when they have done a fair and right thing. It is extremely important for anyone in authority to hear out a matter and investigate a situation before reacting. They may even have to walk away and come before the Lord asking for insight and wisdom before making judgment. This will allow the Spirit of Truth opportunity to search out the matter and reveal angles they may be blind to. A righteous judge considers the evidence and declares judgment considering both sides of the case. Any leader should approach the *bench* with a great sense of responsibility and desire to make a righteous judgment.

ᛒ Observable ᛞ

He that has knowledge spares his words: and a man of understanding is of an excellent spirit. Even a fool, when he holds his peace, is counted wise: and he that shuts his lips is esteemed a man of understanding.

Proverbs 17:27-28

When we are people of understanding we can spare our words. We can hold our peace and shut our lips. In many situations we will be esteemed if we would shut our mouths and direct our thoughts to the Lord rather than speak out all we think or feel.

When we are persons of knowledge we are aware that most of what we would first speak out is not fully thought through. A person of knowledge is one who has taken time to realize they don't know everything and remains in a place to receive instruction.

When we are quiet, we can listen. When we listen, we increase knowledge. When we increase knowledge, we can more properly speak to those things that need our words rather than vent temporary assessments or thoughts.

The next time you find words rushing from your heart to your head, pause and shut your mouth. Consider that the first thing to pop into your mind may not be what the Lord wants out of your mouth.

❧ Desire ❧

Through desire a man will isolate himself; he seeks and intermeddles with all wisdom.

Proverbs 18:1

If a desire is strong enough, it can cause a person to cut off relationships and activities the Lord would have for them. A person can be consumed with fulfilling the desire to the point where other sources of joy and satisfaction are neglected.

We must be cautious with desires. Sometimes the desire can be rooted in the lusts of the flesh, lusts of the eyes or the pride of life. These are of this world and lure us into an unhealthy friendship with the world. Desires have a way of drawing us into pursuits and goals the Lord does not have for us. Soon, we may find ourselves entangled in the affairs of this life.

Our desires are to delight the Lord and be in line with His will for our lives. When we delight ourselves in Him, He will give us the desires of our hearts. He won't only *fulfill* the desires, but He will *place* the *right* desires in our hearts. Our hearts can have longings that are contrary to His plans so we must not trust our own hearts.

He who trusts in his own heart is a fool. Let's seek first His kingdom and His righteousness when a desire finds its way to the surface of our hearts. When we start to break away from certain commitments and relationships due to a desire or longing, let's be sure that the Lord has called us to do this.

ᘒ Self ᘓ

A fool has no delight in understanding, but that his heart may discover itself.

Proverbs 18:2

Our society emphasizes the need for people to understand themselves. I know I am in a constant state of transformation. I am *always* changing. Once I do discover something about myself, I find that it is not worth focusing on. That part of my personality is most likely under construction by the Holy Spirit. I should desire to discover *more* of what He is making me *into* than what I *am* in the present moment.

As we grow in our knowledge of God and *His* ways, we will be transformed by the renewing of our minds. We will take on *His* attributes and *His* heart. These paths of self-discovery, often lead to an inordinate focus on self. If we focus more on what He is making us *into*, which is found in knowing Christ, we have a reference point that never changes. This will allow us to enjoy changes and not seek to understand ourselves, but understand who He is making us into.

ℬ Reputation ℭ

When the wicked comes, then comes also contempt, and with public shame comes reproach.

Proverbs 18:3

Wickedness brings confusion and causes reputations to be marred. Wicked choices and shameful conduct cause others to look upon us with contempt. Even what we do in secret will affect our reputations and examples. A believer is to be honorable and esteemed for directing their life in a way that honors the Lord Jesus Christ and adorns the gospel.

This world is trying to convince people that purity and integrity are things of the past. Many people are choosing wickedness and sin because they think it is necessary to experience life. This is a lie of the devil!

We have the opportunity to shine like *never* before because darkness is encroaching so quickly and strongly. Our life choices should reflect that we believe in a Holy God and His ways. Our reputations will speak to this fallen world change is not only possible, but only possible in Him.

❧ Wellspring ☙

The words of a man's mouth are as deep waters, and
the wellspring of wisdom as a flowing brook.

Proverbs 18:4

What we talk about can provide refreshment for
those who hear us. When we speak words full of life,
we can wash away the stains of depression and
despair from others. As we contribute to a
conversation, our words can redirect the flow away
from cynicism, judgment and anger to a flow of life,
hope and encouragement. In order to have this
effect, our words should be purposed to refresh and
wash away confusion. Opening our mouths with
wisdom is to be a trademark for the virtuous person
whose life has been surrendered to Christ. We must
not be rash with our opinions or quick to speak what
we feel.

We must be people whose words flow forth from a
depth of communication with the Lord. We should
bring matters before Him, praying over them and
hide His word in our hearts. This is the source for
such deep waters and the wellspring of wisdom.

❧ Accolades ☙

It is not good to esteem the person of the wicked, to overthrow the righteous in judgment.

Proverbs 18:5

Awards and accolades are given to all kinds of people in our society for various achievements. Although many of their talents and efforts are of high caliber, we, as believers, must guard our hearts when it comes to esteem and acceptance.

It is not good to accept the person of the wicked. When we admire those who are living or espousing values God defines as wicked, our inner gauges of righteousness can be dulled and confused. A person's popularity should not determine our esteem for them. We can admire talents and gifting that are not associated with wickedness, but once those talents are directly linked to propagating or endorsing wickedness our esteem must not be given. If someone is regarded highly in this world for directly opposing God's standards, they are not to be esteemed but rather prayed for.

A person making a decision based on God's standards, should be esteemed for their obedience. They deserve to be supported and admired.

Lord, help us esteem and accept the things in a person that *You* esteem and accept. Help us be sensitive to any sort of confusion within us in respect to regard or value. Help us see clearly what may be according to the prince of the power of the air and what is rooted in Your eternal truths. In Jesus' name. Amen.

ℬ Destruction ☙

A fool's lips enter into contention, and his mouth calls for strokes. A fool's mouth is his destruction, and his lips are the snare of his soul.

Proverbs 18:6-7

God deals with foolishness. When a person uses his or her mouth to start arguments, God will bring about painful consequences meant to correct. Words have great power and they are to be used carefully. A fool's mouth will bring them down. Whether it is agreeing to do something foolish or speaking things that create havoc and confusion, a fool's mouth brings destruction.

We should avoid using inflammatory words. A fool starts arguments. Our words are to be guided by God who wants to use them for His purposes. We have a wise God who knows what the wise things to say are. If we speak recklessly, we conduct our lives as fools and are promised destruction.

ஐ Wounds ஐ

The words of a talebearer are as wounds, and they go down into the innermost parts of the belly.

Proverbs 18:8

Talebearer is a word many of us aren't familiar with. This is a compound word which means *to bear a tale — to carry a story from one place to another.* The scriptures sometimes refer to this as *repeating a matter.*

When we are in a conversation we should silently ask the Lord whether a story needs to be told. We will sense our Shepherd's leading and know if He has permitted it or whether He is trying to shut the doors of our lips. When we sense a lack of peace, we should leave the story behind. What we may consider an innocent recount of a matter, may have elements within it that could stir up or provoke the other person. There are trigger points, memories, sinful choices and struggles in the hearts with whom we fellowship. We could wound someone without realizing it. If we didn't know someone was allergic to onions and served them, we could create a horrible experience for that person although our hearts were right and our labor was in love. People have histories and we may serve information that could be used by the enemy to kill, steal and destroy.

Be cautious, dear saint. Don't be so quick to speak or share all you know. Listen to His leading and if you sense the Lord trying to stop you, yield and trust He knows best.

ও Waster ল

He also that is lazy in his work is brother to him that is a great waster.

Proverbs 18:9

Most of what makes this world run in the day-to-day happenings involves labor. That's right — work. We must be hard workers. Whether at work, home or in ministry, we cannot be lazy. Something will end up being wasted.

Have you ever seen perfectly good food thrown out because it was left out and reached an unsafe temperature for consumption? The potato salad could have been eaten for another meal or brought to a friend's gathering. Instead, it gets tossed. When we do our work in a lazy way we actually are wasting something.

Sometimes we do half-hearted jobs and end up doing them again. We wasted the time and resources spent on the first attempt. Other times we procrastinate. This may lead to missing out on some other opportunity when the job can no longer be put off. We have wasted the opportunity. When we should do the dishes or repair something in our homes and procrastinate, we might end up having to stay up too late and we waste the sleep we need to wake up ready to live for God.

Oh Lord, show us when we are being lazy in our work. We don't want to waste anything You have for us!

ℬ Tower ℭ

The name of the Lord is a strong tower: the righteous runs into it, and is safe.

Proverbs 18:10

This promise is strengthening. The name of the Lord is a strong tower. His name is a fortress. His name is likened to the highest part of the fortress. His name is a place we can run into and be safe. The key is to run into His name and take refuge there. His name is a strong tower but oftentimes we stand next to it or see it in the distance and don't run into it. We must run into His name — not walk into it, or stroll accidentally into it, but run into it. How do we run into the name of the Lord?

First, we must know His names in order to run into them. The scriptures give us many names of God. He is the Prince of Peace, the Great Shepherd, the Lord of hosts and the Bread of Life. We see Him declared as the Almighty One, the Everlasting Father and the Author and Finisher of our faith. There is a name we can hide in for protection and a vantage point no matter what sort of enemy onslaught is facing us.

Are you familiar with His names? Do you know where the entrance to that strong tower is? It might be helpful to start a journal page with His names and start your time of worship declaring who He is. Here is a list of some of the Old Testament names of God. You can use these *towers* at any time to run into and be safe.

Elohim (God)

If you feel you lack authority in your life.

Jehovah/Yahweh (the self-existent one: I AM)

If you are overwhelmed with the present situation.

Jehovah-jireh (the Lord will provide)

If you are in a place lacking financial provision or help.

Jehovah-rapha (the Lord who heals)

If you or someone you know is wounded or ill spiritually, emotionally or physically.

Jehovah-nissi (the Lord our banner)

If you need to be delivered from a place of defeat and sense the victory you have in Christ.

Jehovah-Shalom (the Lord our peace)

If you are troubled or anxious about anything.

Jehovah-ra-ah (the Lord my shepherd)

If you need to be found, lost your way or intimidated by predators.

Jehovah-tsidkenu (the Lord our righteousness)

If you are feeling condemned or unqualified or have fallen short.

Jehovah-shammad (the Lord is present)

If you have been forsaken or feel like God is not with you.

Jehovah-Elohim (the Lord God)

If you sense other forces trying to impose their authority and influence over a situation.

Jehovah Sabaoth (the Lord of hosts)

If you sense a spiritual battle that is apparent and powerful.

El Elyon (the most high God)

If you sense idolatry in your life or someone else's that is robbing God of His place of supremacy.

Adonai (our master)

If you need direction and orders for your life.

El Shaddai (Almighty God, the strength giver)

If you feel weak and need strength.

El Olam (everlasting God)

If you are facing changes or others' choices are impacting your stability.

These are some of the names of God we can run into and be safe! Ready, set, GO!

❦ Wealth ❧

The rich man's wealth is his strong city, and as a high wall in his own conceit.

Proverbs 18:11

When someone has resources to solve life's problems, they could begin to trust in those resources rather than the One who gave them. When a person has a security system in their home, they might begin to rest peacefully. They could be trusting in the technology that keeps unwanted guests out rather than the One who allowed them the privilege of having such protection.

We see in Job's life, in a moment, that which we enjoy can be taken away. If we find ourselves being provided for or protected today, we should lift up our eyes and worship the One who is behind it all. He is our strong city. He is our shield.

Throughout our days, it would be healthy for us to thank and praise Him for all we consider protection or provision. When we take a sip of coffee, when we put on a seat belt, when we lock the front door, let us thank the Lord for His presence, provision and protection.

❧ Arrogance ☙

*Before destruction the heart of man is arrogant, and
before honor is humility.*

Proverbs 18:12

Our hearts are not to be lifted up. Our hearts need
to be bowed down. We need to be in a place of
constant dependence upon the Lord. Our own
understanding is never to be leaned on. The wisdom
of the Lord can be only be heard by the heart that is
bowed in humility. We can destroy the moment by
having hearts that are arrogant.

Oh that we would be people who are seeking to
please the Lord! We must approach our moments
with a sense of need. Potential conflict should be
confronted with quietness of heart seeking to align
ourselves with His purposes in that moment.

How dare we force upon those around us the
outcome we deem best! Have we not learned that
His ways are higher than ours? Have we not taken
the time to look back and recognize He was working
in difficult situations? Shouldn't we calm ourselves
down, lower our expectations and quietly submit
ourselves to His mind on matters?

Humility brings honor. Arrogance destroys. It is
good to challenge ourselves in most situations by
inwardly saying, *"Maybe, I'm wrong."* We will be
open to correction, leading or affirmation. We will
not cooperate with destruction. We will be
honored.

◎ Answers ◎

He that answers a matter before he hears it, it is foolishness and shame to him.

Proverbs 18:13

"Answering a matter" means giving a response or making a decision. It is coming to a conclusion or saying something based solely on what has been heard up to that point. As people who desire to be wise, this is *not* the way to handle matters. We are not to give an answer before we have all the facts. There are things we can do in order to avoid answering a matter before fully hearing it.

1. *Take what we have heard and bring it before the Lord.*

This would involve bringing what has been said and done before the Lord in intentional prayer. He might show us a missing piece of information or give us discernment of an exaggerated or minimized statement.

2. *Consider all that surrounds a given situation.*

This could involve the time of day, where someone is in the Lord, physical factors that may be at work, cultural influences, age, maturity and other factors. Body position, eye movements and subtle physical responses might be revealing pain, hurt, deception or bitterness.

3. *Ask questions before coming to conclusions.*

A good listener asks for information. These questions may go deeper than the facts and go toward motivations and intentions. Questions should be asked with an honest heart in order to understand.   They should be asked to get information in order to make decisions rooted in truth. They should not be slanted to support any conclusions we might be leaning toward.

Let's be people who hear with more than our ears and refrain our lips from speaking hasty assessments. We will be wise speaking things that are based on more than the first information we receive.

❧ Wounded ☙

The spirit of a man will sustain his infirmity; but a
wounded spirit who can bear?

Proverbs 18:14

When someone is wounded deep within, they are
not always the easiest to be around. They are
difficult to bear. People lose the courage to go on
when they have a wounded spirit. Many
relationships may become affected by one wound.
Some of us have been there and some of us have
known those in such a place.

We must guard our spirits when we are wounded so
we have the strength to make it through the healing
process. We need strength to bring our injured souls
before the Word of God. This will enable us to
discern the greater good the Lord is seeking to
accomplish in the situation. Nurturing the wound
will contribute to its painful impact and might cause
it to penetrate deeper than necessary.

Our spirits must stay in constant fellowship with
God who loves us. We shouldn't allow the sins of
others to contaminate our safe place. Their sin has
no bearing on God's love and favor toward us. From
the beginning the devil has sought to interrupt the
fellowship man has with God. In the Garden of
Eden, we see Satan jealous of the ongoing fellowship
man had with God. He deceives Eve and we find
Adam and Eve hiding from God. Our spirits will
sustain our infirmities and must not remain
wounded and hidden from the mercies of God.

Approach the Lord with your pain and don't hide
from Him. Don't allow wounds to drive you into
hiding. We need to be before Him and in Him while
we are wounded. This will allow us to continue

enjoying our relationships with God, our children, our spouses and others no matter what sort of wounds we have experienced.

❧ Acquire ☙

The heart of the prudent gets knowledge; and the ear of the wise seeks knowledge.

Proverbs 18:15

In order to become wise people, we must get and seek. People are good at *getting* and *seeking*. Sometimes we want to get that new outfit or seek the best deal. The Lord has placed within us a desire to go after things. The problem is what things are we going after? We need to *get* wisdom and we need to *seek* knowledge.

We are to humble ourselves and realize the knowledge we have is not enough. We are ill-equipped at times. We shouldn't get frustrated. We must position ourselves like we would to go shopping. If we needed to purchase something we would not necessarily dread it. We would go out there looking for the item looking forward to owning something new. The search for the item can be challenging and enjoyable.

If we need knowledge about something we must look to His Word, godly counsel, pastoral teaching and prayer as if shopping. Just as we usually don't buy the first thing we see, we should shop wisdom until we find the answer that we believe God is giving us.

Lord, help us not panic when we lack knowledge but know you lay up sound wisdom for the righteous. If we seek we will find.

℘ Opportunities ℘

A man's gift makes room for him, and brings him before great men.

Proverbs 18:16

Our culture tries to convince us that we have to make our own way. We are taught to be assertive and draw attention to our strengths. The Lord's way is different. We are to focus on serving Him and be faithful in all He asks us to do. He will use the gifts He has placed in us to bring us into opportunities.

Our opinions of how we should be used are corrupted and biased. We must focus on being faithful to use whatever the Lord has given us in a way that is diligent and unto Him. He will spotlight us in His timing. He has works foreordained for us to walk in. We are to be people who seek to serve the Lord and not seek recognition or favor from man. The Lord brings promotion and the Lord assigns His people to the works *He* wants them to do.

He knows when we are mature or spiritually-equipped enough for the tasks He has for us to do. If we take the higher seat in a situation and the Lord has not bid us to come, we could end up falling off of it. We might sustain serious spiritual injuries and unnecessary wounds and pain. We don't see as He sees and we are not to tell the Master what His servant should be doing.

Let's be aware of the gifts He has given us. Let's be willing to use them in secret. The Lord who sees in secret will exalt us in due time.

ဆ Natural ‌‌ങ

He that is first in his own cause seems just; but his
neighbor comes and questions him.

Proverbs 18:17

This bit of wisdom not only works for parents trying
to sift through the muddled cries of conflict between
their children, but this counsel is an excellent
warning for sifting through our own internal
conflicts as well.

Our first thoughts are not to be trusted. We can
quickly come to conclusions and deem them as *just*
responses. These conclusions feel natural and give
us a sense of direction. The Holy Spirit can be a
neighbor that comes and questions us. He will
search us out and affirm or challenge what we have
decided to do.

It is natural to consider our instincts as the way we
should go because they are most likely rooted in the
familiar. We, like Abraham, must be open to leaving
a familiar land of response and go to a new land of
reaction. We, like Peter, might have to leave the
boat, and walk on that which we have never walked
on before. We, like Gideon, might have to approach
a battle with less resources than we would naturally
think we need. We, like David, may have to dwell in
the wilderness and still believe it is the king's
habitation. We, like the woman with the issue of
blood, may have to break through our religious and
cultural boundaries to reach out and receive from
the Lord.

That which may seem right in our own eyes, must be
brought before the Judge who judges righteously
and request His judgment.

❧ Chance ❧

The lot causes contentions to cease, and parts between the mighty.

Proverbs 18:18

Passion and conviction bring men to a place where a decision must be made but no one is willing to compromise. This could result in division and oh, how the enemy likes to use division to accomplish his goals! When we are in a place where there is not necessarily a right or wrong but rather strong preference, the casting of the lots might do us well to cease division and get on with life. "Casting lots" means to do some sort of procedure where chance alone dictates the outcome. Flipping a coin, choosing which hand has the coin and drawing straws are all forms of casting lots.

The Lord does not want us casting lots when His Word and Spirit speak clearly to a situation. Chance can be used when there is division between people because of preference. When two children run for the same toy, a mother could flip a coin for who is first and then set a time limit for the next player. A mother would most likely not be blamed for showing favorites in this case. Another good method for splitting portions of food is to let one person divide the portion and the other one gets to pick first which portion to consume. Casting lots is not the way to run our lives but definitely comes in handy at times of contention.

๛ Offended cs

A brother offended is harder to be won than a strong city: and their contentions are like the bars of a castle.

Proverbs 18:19

A strong city is a walled city. It is surrounded by walls able to resist penetration. These walls have towers in which watchmen are always on alert for impending attack. When someone is offended and has not forgiven they are like this city. They begin to build walls and keep a fortified distance between their heart and passersby. They are on alert anticipating hostile relationships and their defenses are up. Their justifications for their personality change are many and well built like bars on a castle. This person is hard to connect with and oftentimes easily defensive.

There are people like this in our lives and we mustn't give up on them. Even if we find ourselves not connecting with them, we should pray for an opening into the walls of their city. When we find it, we should connect in conversation and concern. Some of their anger may be rooted in a past offense. We should see them through their social awkwardness and be committed to loving them. We must pray that they will forgive and show them that kind of love.

We are warned to not be like this offended brother. Has a past offense created walls behind which you hide? Are you missing out on new relationships and memories? The enemy wants us to be isolated. He knows this makes us vulnerable, stubborn and not fit for the Master's use.

Lord, show us if we have built these walls and help us to forgive from the heart. Help us to remember that as You, God, were in Christ Jesus forgiving us, we, from the heart must forgive one another.

ଚ Kill ଓ

A man's belly shall be satisfied with the fruit of his mouth; and with the increase of his lips shall he be filled. Death and life are in the power of the tongue: and they that love it shall eat the fruit thereof.

Proverbs 18:20-21

We will eat the words we speak. What we say, when we say it and with whom we speak all affect what our lives will be filled with. God wants us to be satisfied and He instructs us that our words greatly determine the quality of life we experience.

Death and life are in the power of the tongue. We can use our words to kill and we can use them to bring life.

There are things we are to kill. There are things we shouldn't. We can use our words to slay gossip and demand the conversation change. We can use words to kill joy in someone by murmuring and complaining.

Our words can bring life. We can speak in a way that revives the weary soul. We can flirt with someone and bring romantic feelings to life that should not live.

The prophets were sent to speak God's Word to *"To destroy and to throw down, to build and to plant."* (Jer 1:10) May our words kill what God would have them kill and bring alive that which should live.

ဢ Wives ಣ

Whoever finds a wife finds a good thing, and obtains favor of the Lord.

Proverbs 18:22

When a man finds a wife, he finds a good thing. Women are good things! Our accuser of the brethren wants women to focus on their failures. Perhaps he wants women to focus on the shortcomings of their figures, cooking or parenting skills. Ladies, we must start out with this truth. If our husbands have found us, they have found a good thing. Sure, we can get better, but let's remember this starting point. Brothers, remember that no matter how many shortcomings your wife may have, God says that she is a *good* thing. Maybe wives should text husbands like this:

Please pick up some milk at the store.

I love you,

Love,

A.G.T. (a good thing)

Another great part of this verse is that husbands obtain favor from the Lord by having a wife. Why? How? I don't know, but I believe it because this verse says it. Perhaps the opportunity to have marital relations frees husbands up from so much of the struggle of the flesh that He can hear the Lord more. Perhaps the wisdom that wives share brings balance and insight causing the two to have a better return for their efforts. It might be that he has someone to pray for him and with him. Maybe it is being able to bounce things off of his wife and work through his thoughts verbally with someone who is for him and not against him. Whatever it is, a wife could text like this:

Please pick up bread for lunches.

I love you.

Glad I could help you obtain favor from the Lord.

Love,

Your Good Thing

ಉ Impoverished ೮

The poor uses humble requests; but the rich answers roughly.

Proverbs 18:23

A poor man will ask for mercy but a rich man will answer harshly. We are rich in many ways. We can start searching for answers within our own resources before seeking God. Blessed are the poor in spirit for theirs is the kingdom of God. No matter how *rich* we think we are in experience, knowledge, money, time or resources, we are absolutely impoverished in comparison to God who is rich in mercy, wisdom and judgment. We must face the most common difficulty asking for His mercy and resources. He might use something He has already given us, but He knows what is needed more than we ever could.

❧ Friendly ☙

A man that has friends must show himself friendly:
and there is a friend that sticks closer than a brother.

Proverbs 18:24

When we become consumed with how many friends we have, our focus becomes trying to *be* a friend. We may end up in commitments that compete with our first love relationship with the Lord. We *must* show ourselves friendly with many friends. We can only be good friends when we focus first on our friendship with the Lord. Our daily times with Him, our trust in Him, our desire to cultivate relationship with Him and grow in our knowledge of Him, must be our priority. We should be making new memories with Him as well.

Our friendship with Christ should be our priority or we might be people who are pulled by the expectations of others. We will lose our ability to properly assess our priorities. When we focus on people for our worth or value, we quickly lose our bearings and end up showing ourselves *friendly*.

Let's reevaluate our friendship with Christ and be sure that our loyalty to Him exceeds our loyalty to any human relationship.

Made in the USA
San Bernardino, CA
12 August 2017